Premiere Events

Library Programs That Inspire

Premiere Events: Library Programs That Inspire Elementary School Patrons. By Patricia Potter Wilson and Roger Leslie.

Center Stage: Library Programs That Inspire Middle School Patrons. By Patricia Potter Wilson and Roger Leslie. (forthcoming)

Igniting the Spark: Library Programs That Inspire High School Patrons. By Roger Leslie and Patricia Potter Wilson. (forthcoming)

Premiere Events

Library Programs That Inspire Elementary School Patrons

Patricia Potter Wilson
and
Roger Leslie

2001
Libraries Unlimited, Inc.
Englewood, Colorado

*To Uncle Son and Jerry in appreciation
for their loving support*

LIBRARIES UNLIMITED, INC.
P.O. Box 6633
Englewood, CO 80155-6633
1-800-237-6124
www.lu.com

Library of Congress Cataloging-in-Publication Data

Wilson, Patricia J. (Patricia Jane)
    Premiere events : library programs that inspire elementary school patrons / Patricia
Potter Wilson and Roger J. Leslie.
        p. cm.
    Includes bibliographical references and index.
    ISBN 1-56308-795-2
    1. Elementary school libraries--Activity programs. 2. Media programs (Education)
I. Leslie, Roger. II. Title.

Z675.S3 W7545 2001
027.62'5--dc21

                                                                          2001018614

Contents

Chapter 1
HOW AND WHY PROGRAMS REALLY WORK (*continued*)

Chapter 2
INITIAL STAGES OF PROGRAM PLANNING 23

Chapter 3
FINAL STAGES OF PROGRAM PLANNING 43

Chapter 8
DYNAMIC MODEL PROGRAMS AND IDEAS

List of Figures

Acknowledgments

We want to express our gratitude to the school library media specialists, university professors, and friends who supported us throughout this project. First, we want thank the 20 library media specialists who provided the model programs and ideas that are shared in Chapter 8. Without their wonderful program ideas, there would be no book, as their section is the heart of this particular how-to guide. It is our hope that other school library media specialists will want to try these programs in their own library media centers.

The professors in the School of Education at the University of Houston—Clear Lake shared generously of their time and knowledge. Their patience with constant questioning, their sharing of ideas, and their enthusiasm for the project are much appreciated.

Ms. Ann Kimzey, Dr. Ken Black, and Dr. Maureen White were always there to advise us and provide the support we needed. Their encouragement and confidence in our project are sincerely appreciated. The book could never have been completed without the technological skills of Mr. Isidro Grau; the secretarial skills of Mrs. Vera Fluker; and the support of Jerry Roberts, Dora Rhodes, and Wendell Wilson. Their dedication to the project is much appreciated. We particularly want to thank Julie Hardegree and Kit Chiu for the numerous hours they spent searching the Internet for outstanding Web sites.

Although many school library media specialists were involved in this project, we want to extend a special thank you to the University of Houston—Clear Lake students who completed their School Library and Information Science internships during the summer of 1999. They worked diligently, examining model programs in various school districts. We also want to thank Dr. Barry Bishop, Kay McBride, Jay Stailey, and Sarah Wahl for providing us with so much support throughout the project.

Finally, we want to extend our sincere gratitude to our project editor, Rich Lane at Libraries Unlimited, who was always available to answer our numerous questions. His commitment to the project made the whole thing work. Never too busy to discuss the project or answer questions, Rich spent much time on the telephone and through e-mail discussing the book with us and refining our chapters.

Introduction

I could not have been happier with the success of *Happenings: Developing Successful Programs for School Libraries* (Libraries Unlimited, 1987). Even after the book went out of print following a lengthy run, I continued to receive notes and calls from users requesting "more, more." Inspired by the responses and suggestions, my co-author, Roger Leslie, and I decided to offer much more than a mere update of *Happenings* and instead set out to provide a new series of books to address the unique needs of librarians at all three education levels: elementary, middle, and high school.

Although *Premiere Events* targets elementary library media specialists and district library coordinators, it is designed to be equally valuable to district administrators who work with school libraries and to the increasing number of principals discovering how vital media centers are to the success of a school. Additionally, although the major focus is school library media centers, we think the book can also help support public librarians in program development for elementary-age patrons.

The core information of this book draws on our own extensive backgrounds as school library media specialists. As a former elementary media specialist, I was an avid program developer. My principal, Marilyn Coker McPhillips, and I shared similar educational philosophies. In acknowledging the importance of the school library media center as the heart of the school, I immediately recognized the educational and public relations benefits derived from sponsoring special programs in the library. As I browsed various library resources in search of program ideas and professional works that could help me create my own library programs, I became aware of the lack of resources on the topic. Although there were some works on specific types of programs, such as Carolyn Feller Bauer's resources that focus on programming with children's literature and Joni Bodart's *Booktalk* series, there were few books that addressed programs in general. After developing and presenting numerous programs in my own school library media center and attending programs in various school and public libraries, I wrote *Happenings*.

Later, after receiving a doctorate in education and becoming a university professor who teaches school library courses, I realized the importance of emphasizing library program development when preparing future school librarians. In my role as university educator, I added a programming component to the school library administration course as well as to the internship. In my role as internship supervisor, I have enjoyed the privilege of visiting numerous school library media centers and observing some stellar programs firsthand.

My co-author, Roger Leslie, is a secondary media specialist with a solid understanding of elementary libraries. Juggling three careers as writer, book reviewer, and media specialist provides him with a rich background from which to create programs. His work as a novelist and screenwriter puts him in contact with artists from both fields, whose guest appearances are a favorite of students at his school. Reviewing young adult books for *Booklist* gives him firsthand knowledge of resource topics of interest to young patrons and of forthcoming publishing trends that provide an immediacy to programs children attend. Finally, his daily work with students keeps him in touch with their interests, needs, and personalities, all key factors in appropriately shaping a library program to its audience.

The purpose of this book is fourfold: (1) to provide detailed information concerning how to plan, execute, and assess school library programs; (2) to emphasize the benefits reaped from such programs; (3) to provide services to enrich programs; and (4) to share winning program ideas that were developed and carried out by award-winning elementary media specialists across the nation.

Our major goal is to motivate media specialists to create programs. These programs will inspire young patrons to read books and use the library media center. They will also prove invaluable avenues for supporting and enriching the curriculum as well as addressing the personal interests of students and faculty. Finally, they will provide a way to advertise and promote both the school and the school library.

CHAPTER BY CHAPTER PREVIEW

Chapter 1 begins with an example of a successful program that I planned and executed in my own elementary school library media center some years ago. Through this example and the subsequent discussion, the chapter provides a diverse working definition of the terms *library programming* and *library programs.* Further, it specifies the need for their routine use in developing an effective library, as well as the ongoing benefits perpetuated by library programs.

Chapter 2 focuses on the idea stage of programming. Although sometimes the most difficult stage of the entire process, it is often the most essential. The best librarians know what interests all patrons, including students at each grade level and the faculty. Beyond discovering patron interest through random requests, the librarian needs some simple but effective tools for assessing the needs, concerns, and curiosities of students and teachers. Chapter 2 provides those tools.

Chapter 3 describes the various steps necessary for planning and organizing a successful library program. A veritable how-to manual for librarians, this chapter offers librarians a clear, step-by-step template for creating a variety of programs.

Chapter 4 provides information about where and how to locate resources that will enrich your programs. Beyond the predictable avenues, Chapter 4 also suggests some frequently overlooked but impressively worthwhile places to find the support media specialists will need to execute program plans.

Chapter 5 discusses how to organize the resources. Various sample forms are provided to help you organize special programs. Where and how to find volunteers and support staff is also highlighted.

Beyond the community resources immediately available to library media specialists is another invaluable tool literally at their fingertips: the Internet. Chapter 6 offers a list of Internet sites related to many subjects and areas of interest to children. Additionally, it includes Web sites of particular interest to educators, as well as sites that connect media specialists to material resources that enhance programming.

Because assessment and evaluation are an essential phase of any library program, Chapter 7 recommends various ways to discern the strengths and weaknesses of programs. More important, it goes a step further to help library media specialists enhance and rejuvenate good programs they want to repeat and refine or eliminate programs that no longer meet students' needs.

The heart of the book is Chapter 8, which presents some of the best programs currently being offered in school library media centers across the nation. Each program highlights the most creative and successful efforts from experts, often award-winning library media specialists. In hopes of addressing as many readers' interests and needs as possible, the sample programs are intended for all audiences, including students, teachers, and even parents.

Five appendixes support the text with a program survey, a full model program, a sample of student and educator activities, a rich resources list, and a topical bibliography to spur more programming ideas.

We hope that *Premiere Events* does more than merely pique your interest in programming. Instead, our intent is to stir your creative energy and inspire you to have a more profound impact on student learning than before. Although many responsibilities of library media specialists lead to meaningful teaching opportunities, personal experience has convinced us that nothing creates a dynamic learning environment quite like a well-executed school library media program.

CHAPTER 1

How and Why Programs Really Work

Not long ago I experienced one of those magical teaching moments only those of us involved in education can fully appreciate. I watched as my four guest speakers held students spellbound and excited about their learning throughout a library program that I had developed. As I stood at the exit of my school library media center and thanked students for their participation, I was inundated with enthusiastic comments:

"I want to be a pilot, too."

"Do you have books on Japanese foods?"

"I want to learn more about origami. It's fun!"

"Sayonara," the last student bowed respectfully, then flashed a huge smile as he raced to catch up with the rest of his class.

This additional feedback only solidified what I had discovered in the process of my work: Library programs are dynamic tools worth incorporating into the core duties of being an effective school library media specialist.

Until recently, even library science courses provided only cursory information about programming. Consequently, early in my career I had thought of programs as activities beyond my regular duties. When I had extra time, I decided, I could incorporate a special event that made the students, parents, and administrators more aware of the library media center. I quickly discovered that extra time is never available.

Undaunted, I set out to do programs. In the exciting but often hectic weeks of preparing a program with no guidelines, I often wondered if such events really made much difference to my patrons or to my professional success. Through experience I discovered that programming is the very lifeblood of an effective school library media center.

Immediately after my first two-day program, book circulation increased resoundingly, and media that had never seen the light of a classroom were being requested so frequently I had to make a waiting list.

Parents who initially intended to share only two days of their time to help with the program signed up for permanent stints as weekly volunteers. And for once, I alone was not having to come up with new public relations ploys to generate interest in my school library media center. The program, "The Culture of Japan," set off a ripple effect in the school and the community that continued for several gratifying weeks.

Was my program an elaborate extravaganza that strained my budget, frayed my nerves, and whittled away weeks of my life? Not at all. If anything, it was a multifaceted yet relatively simple program. Capitalizing on the learning center technique that is familiar to elementary classrooms but seldom used in the media center, I created a program made up of four separate centers, each related to my theme, "The Culture of Japan":

Travel: A Flight to Tokyo

Culture: A Japanese Celebration

Art: Fun with Origami

Cooking: How to Make and Eat Rice Balls

The two-day program highlighted local experts in each field who generously shared their time and knowledge with our elementary youngsters. As event facilitator, I devised a schedule that allowed every student in grades four and five to visit each center. The guest speakers assembled their displays within the confines of their assigned center and planned a 20-minute presentation to be repeated five times each day to groups of approximately 25 students.

The school library media center became a spectacular exhibit hall that the students relished. Displays hanging from the ceiling were the focus of the first center, "A Flight to Tokyo." Directing this flight of model airplanes was a commercial airline pilot who set the tone for the international passage to Tokyo by wearing his uniform and displaying navigation charts and models of aircraft. While guiding the captivated students toward their descent, he unfurled a dazzling aerial photograph of Tokyo. They had arrived on the other side of the world. As the students left this center, the pilot gave them their very own pilot wings as a remembrance of their journey.

Mrs. Hirumi, dressed in her kimono, bowed and greeted students as they entered the second center, decorated to introduce children to her native Japan. Setting the stage with a huge, colorful map behind her and paper lanterns cascading around the parameter of her center, Hirumi enlivened the voyage with details of her own family's traditions. As she shared photographs and her personal memories of childhood, such as schooling, recreation, and holiday celebrations, the students sat spellbound.

With great dexterity, the children grasped the concept of the intricate origami activity in the third center. The artist invited youngsters to participate in her demonstration of paper folding as she introduced them to Ed Young's *A Thousand Paper Cranes*. (Due to time allotments she was unable to read the book to the class, but she promised that it would be the focus of the media specialist's next read-aloud.) During her demonstration, the fourth- and fifth-grade artists eagerly creased their paper into exotic cranes. Some students took their creations home; others opted to leave their masterpieces in the school library media center to become part of a permanent display.

The sweet aroma of rice permeated the air in the last center. A traditional table was decorated and set with bowls and chopsticks. Each child was given a large spoon of cooked rice to shape into a ball and eat as the chef demonstrated how to make Japanese rice balls. After her demonstration, children were given a recipe for rice balls to take home to their parents.

Because detailed scheduling and steady traffic flow were paramount to this program's success, the teachers, volunteers, and I were busy stagehands during the two days of presentations. For the remainder of the week, the displays remained intact, and eager volunteers continued to take part in the event. Although most monitored the students who wanted to browse through the centers or check out displayed books related to the topics, several volunteers continued to demonstrate the art of origami.

During the event, the school principal and district administrators visited, fellow library media specialists dropped by, and a reporter from the local newspaper took photographs and wrote a short article. Word of the event filtered throughout the district, and soon school library media center programming became the best public relations for my school library media center, especially because it inspired more students to pay regular visits. I had engaged my young patrons by showing them, firsthand, that the school library media center is a vibrant, exciting place in which to learn.

MEDIA CENTER PROGRAMMING DEFINED

Although the special activities described above provide a clear example of a school library media center program, it is by no means definitive. In general, a program can be almost any special event or "happening" in the school library media center. Such events usually consist of a planned activity or activities that are organized and executed to fulfill a predefined set of goals. Encompassed under this broad description is an array of possibilities, ranging from simple displays or one-speaker presentations to elaborate, week-long events open to the school population and the community. In any form, media center programs are created to serve the needs of students and faculty. Done well, they will simultaneously engender a positive mindset about school library media centers, encourage patrons to frequent the media center more often, and increase the use and circulation of resources. Media specialists usually call the entire body of their work responsibility their "school library media center program," but throughout this text the words *program* and *programming* refer exclusively to special events created by media specialists.

WHAT LIBRARY MEDIA SPECIALISTS SAY ABOUT PROGRAMMING

"Programs in the media center keep the school and the library media center really exciting for children."

"School library programs can spark a student's curiosity, build on students' interests, inform our patrons of new ideas and information and enhance curriculum."

"Programs provide enrichment—something special for the school community."

These statements were made by school library media specialists at the elementary level in response to a question on a survey: "Why do you feel library programs are important?"

A survey consisting of 10 questions related to school library programming was sent to 20 school library media specialists at the elementary level, who were invited to contribute exemplary programs to this book. The media specialists were selected for the project based on the following criteria: The media specialist was a recipient of the School Librarian of the Year Award for the state, served as president of a state school library association, and/or was recommended by a state or district school library media director.

The survey defined a *school library program* as "a special event planned by the media specialist." The program could include guest speakers, learning centers, demonstrations, displays, or exhibits that could take place in the school library media center or at another site. The survey is in Appendix A.

When asked how frequently they did programming, only four respondents stated that they did it often. Fourteen indicated "sometimes," and two said that they did it seldom. When identifying the content areas on which their library programs most frequently focus, 16 of the 20 pointed to language arts/reading, two said computer technology, and two noted professional development.

Media specialists were asked: "What is the biggest problem you face when planning and presenting a library program?" According to 14 of the media specialists, lack of time for planning and implementation was the greatest problem. The others pointed to scheduling programs within the time constraints of instructional time and lack of personnel and volunteers to help with programs.

Media specialists went on to identify the "major rewards derived from developing a library program." The majority of the media specialists mentioned two or three. The following rewards are ranked by frequency of mention:

1. Enrichment for students

2. Promoting lifelong reading

3. The pleasure that students exhibited when they participated in programs

4. Praise and gratitude from teachers

5. Public relations with students, parents, and community

Other benefits also mentioned were:

- Receive funding for technology and print materials due to programs offered
- Make the media center a visible, integral part of the community
- Build interest in services and materials
- "The most important reward I can receive are these words: 'Thank you for a job well done.'"

The monetary support for the programs comes from the following four sources, in rank order:

1. Book fairs

2. PTO or PTA

3. Principals

4. Grants

Fifteen of the twenty media specialists said that they received support from their principals. Some even said their principals took part in suggesting ideas as well as funding and promoting the programs. They also went on to say that the success of the programs depends on collaboration with their teachers. They mentioned that their teachers often provide suggestions for presenters and work together with them. Comments related to collaboration with teachers included the following:

"Developing library programs is a team effort."

"Collaboration is very important and the greatest benefit for the students takes place when teachers are involved."

"Teachers become the PR people as I support them."

"On a monthly basis, I meet separately with teachers of each grade level to help integrate various materials into the curriculum. At these meetings, I can determine teacher needs and share with them information about materials available in the school library media center. If I'm planning any special activities, teachers are good at suggesting ideas appropriate for a special age level." (see Photo 1.1)

Photo 1.1. Media specialist Betty Anne Smith frequently attends grade-level meetings and collaborates with teachers concerning curricular needs and program activities. *(Royall Elementary School, Florence, South Carolina, Florence School District One)*

From the results of the survey, it became evident that, despite the restrictions their daily routines impose upon their time, school library media specialists who incorporated programming into their schedules immediately recognized the power and effectiveness of them. Even better, they were able to experience firsthand the rich rewards of sharing with students a special event that made a clear and significant impact on learning.

TYPES OF PROGRAMS

Perhaps the greatest advantage of school library media center programs is their flexibility. Media specialists can select from a variety of program types to address the interests of their students, fulfill the curricular needs of their schools, and accommodate their own expertise. These types come in various formats, or program designs, that can meet different needs and interests. By first determining learners' needs and setting program goals, the media specialist will discover which formats logically match those goals. Choosing a single format then becomes a matter of personal taste. Just as important, the format can easily be changed in subsequent years to meet different students' needs or simply to provide the media specialist with a fresh approach. Detailed descriptions and specific examples of the various program types are included in Chapter 2.

Exhibits and Displays

Often the most eye-catching and long-lasting programs are built around displays. At its most rudimentary, this type of program can be a simple display of books. From there, elaboration can add vitality. Selecting books on related topics or themes can be enhanced by a bulletin board sporting an intriguing title or by charts and exhibit items that pique curiosity. A locked display case provides an opportunity to add more valuable, and more attractive, ornamentation to the display while also serving as a more permanent fixture of the library. With less risk of damage or dust, the display can remain for as long as the exhibit is timely and effective. To meet specific program needs, various types of exhibits and displays are possible, including free-standing exhibits, table displays, poster exhibits, and shelf displays.

Featured Speakers or Entertainers

Frequently, media specialists call on one or more guest speakers to share knowledge on a topic of interest. In such cases, the media specialist's main responsibility is to accommodate the needs of the speaker, who generally will bring materials and will need only the space and, occasionally, the equipment to make a presentation. Naturally, resources associated with the topic or written by the guest author must be ordered well in advance and processed for immediate availability to students.

Learning Centers

Because they are both attractive and effective, learning centers are a staple of most elementary classrooms. For these same reasons, they are also being used more frequently in school library media centers. Elaborate partitioned areas intended to divide large groups, as well as simple individual centers set up on a table or study carrel, both serve the same purpose: They provide students with an opportunity to participate in a hands-on activity to grasp a concept, develop a skill, or discover a new tool for learning.

Demonstrations

Often the favorite of students because of their hands-on design, these programs can be facilitated by a teacher, the media specialist, or an expert from outside the school. This format allows for more interactive learning for students. As the instructor gives the demonstration, students can observe, model the behavior, or even ask questions. Whether presented by someone who works at the school or by a guest from the community, the guidelines that apply to a guest speaker also apply here.

Media

Although media presentations are frequently used in conjunction with a program of some other format, events can be built exclusively around a video, slide show, recording, computer program, or multimedia presentation. Because young people naturally gravitate to the familiar, presentations that mirror their recreational activities (watching television, playing computer games) will attract them and, done well, will hold their attention.

Within every program type is the freedom for media specialists to be as simple or sophisticated as they like. Even more advantageous is the opportunity to expand or restrict any program as needed. Popular book displays can evolve into elaborate multimedia centers. Conversely, huge, extravagant events can be cut down to simple demonstration areas or learning centers that can remain intact while student interest persists.

FRAMEWORKS FOR PREPARING A PROGRAM

Just as types of programs vary markedly, so do the frameworks within which any type of program might be presented. Every successful program begins with a focus that determines its framework. That focus can be based on several factors essential to providing the best service to students, the faculty, and the community.

Programs Based on
Specific Target Groups

Because providing a service to an audience is the primary purpose of a program, a logical program type is one intended for a specific group within the student population. Choosing such a group should prove a manageable challenge. Although most people recognize media specialists' organizational talents, they seldom appreciate a much more valuable skill: Successful media specialists know the interests of each segment of their student body. Although this skill is developed to purchase resources that meet student requests and needs, it is an invaluable element of deciding what programs are appropriate for different groups.

Media specialists can choose any group as the target for a program. The sample programs in Chapter 8 illustrate that media specialists can select as broad an audience as the entire student body or any subgroup within the school. Whether targeting students in a specific grade, a school club, or even special populations (gifted and talented, special education), the media specialist has boundless avenues for selecting a group that could benefit from a program custom-made for them. For example, an innovative colleague of mine, Rose Maxwell, recently hosted a school library media center program about pet care that targeted only kindergarten and first-grade students. Because she knew her primary school children loved to read about animals, the topic choice was perfect. Although keeping the information appropriately simple for her target audience, she invited a local veterinarian to discuss the importance of caring for pets. Clearly, targeting a group does not limit a program. Instead, it clarifies its framework so the program can more specifically meet the audience's needs.

Programs Based on Curriculum Needs

In the school setting, many programs will naturally be created to enhance curriculum. Fortunately, even here tremendous flexibility is afforded the media specialist. Although some standard curriculum allows modifying and honing programs that can be repeated, the ever-evolving demands of new state and national standards ensure that media specialists will always have opportunities to develop programs based on fresh new curricular requirements. Curriculum guides from language arts/reading, math, science, and social studies offer voluminous ideas for developing a program. Media specialist Lynn Wendleson showed fifth-grade students a more personal dimension to a space-related science unit by constructing a free-standing exhibit, "Women in Space," that proved so popular, she developed an entire presentation to build on her original idea.

Programs Based on a Special Theme

Because of its specific parameters, a thematic program is often the easiest to develop. Whether the theme is dictated by district demands (multicultural or technology fairs) or special events (World Series or Olympics), such programs offer the freedom to explore and develop that theme creatively. Best of all, creative expression need not be squelched by having to focus too long on making logistical decisions (for example, which groups to invite) because most of these decisions are dictated by the theme itself. Because the theme usually determines the what and when of the program, planning evolves around finding the most fun, effective way of presenting the theme. Picking up on the "Bring a Pet Photo to School" activity that was sponsored by the third-grade teachers, a media specialist in California expanded the theme into the school library media center, where photographs of favorite pets were displayed according to various categories (for example, snakes, dogs, cats, and hamsters) along with the available resources on pets.

Programs Based on Interest and Entertainment

Flexibility, variety, and fun are the driving forces behind these programs. With entertainment as the major objective, media specialists are likely to find that student enthusiasm for the event adds to the satisfaction of nurturing students' personal needs. Best of all, learning occurs within the larger context of student pleasure. In one example, participating in a magic show sponsored by the library, students developed motor skills, sharpened hand/eye coordination, and were even introduced to the abstract concepts of illusion. Drawn in by their own curiosity and enjoyment, the students enthusiastically engaged in firsthand learning, and in the end requested more information from the school library media center on magic tricks.

Programs Based on Available Time Periods

Clearly, time will be an important factor in developing a program. The amount of time available or the time period during which the program takes place affects the type of program that can be designed. Like all aspects of programming, the parameters for a time-based program are still limitless. The range may vary from a one-time, 30-minute event to a program that evolves and is ongoing throughout the entire year. Commonly, short-term programs that involve guest speakers may become routine parts of the school year. Special events such as the World Series and Super Bowl provide program topics on a yearly basis. Programs that students may come to anticipate each year could include a fall festival in

October; a Christmas, Hanukkah, or Kwanzaa program in December; or a book fair in the spring.

PURPOSES OF PROGRAMS

Media specialists who develop programs for elementary students and teachers begin with a specific purpose in mind. At this level, the most common goals of any media center program is to support and enhance the curriculum, enrich students' personal interests, or provide professional growth for teachers.

Support and Enhance the Curriculum

Naturally, the primary function of any school facility focuses on curriculum. With the wealth of resources available, responsibility to provide support through the school library media center weighs heavily on media specialists. Primary focus must be centered on subjects in the core curriculum (reading/language arts, social studies, science, and math). Also essential at the elementary level are special programs that round out the students' education. Once relegated merely to music and physical education, this category now encapsulates many fascinating fields, including visual arts, multicultural studies, technology, and unique programs directed at either gifted or special education students. Because media specialists must be familiar with the curriculum of each grade level, they already have the background needed to plan programs for students of any grade. During an interview, a South Carolina media specialist explained that she examines the math, science, and social studies textbooks for each grade level to acquaint herself with the content of each subject. She also copies the tables of contents from each textbook and files them at the front of her "program planning" drawer, and they are the first reference she uses to develop a new program.

Reading/Language Arts Curriculum

Because reading and writing make up much of the elementary classroom day, the language arts teacher and media specialist share a close bond. Students frequently depend on their media specialist to help them locate books and materials that fulfill their need for information and recreational reading. Through special programs related to the language arts, media specialists provide rich experiences that supplement the language arts classroom and encourage lifelong learning.

Favorite programs related to language arts include visits by children's authors and illustrators. High-profile celebrities like Jan Brett or Eric Carle, who have national reputations for their children's books, create fabulous PR for any school library media center. Often, however, famous authors' speaking fees are too high for many school budgets.

Fortunately, many less-known writers are outstanding and affordable. First-time authors especially can be an ideal find. In hopes of jump-starting their careers, they often work the hardest to meet program needs while charging the least. Some will forego a fee entirely just for the chance to share their work and establish some name recognition in the community. In any of these cases, if children go away from the presentations eager to read, the program is a success.

Other types of programs that typically support the language arts curriculum and that children love include booktalks, read-alouds, story-telling, and story apron activities. In one school in Colorado Springs, second-grade students eagerly await Friday afternoons when grand-parents read aloud in the library. At another school, fifth-graders look forward to sharing their own stories with first-graders during the story-telling program each January. One media specialist's success with creating story aprons to go along with favorite picture books was contagious. After using a story apron to present Eric Carle's *The Very Hungry Caterpillar*, the second-grade teachers followed her lead and began using the story apron concept in place of their flannel boards for sharing good stories. See Appendix C for more information about story aprons.

Because creating lifelong readers is a primary objective of all media specialists, language arts programs are the most frequently developed. Chapter 8 highlights many more exciting program ideas that support the language arts curriculum.

Social Studies Curriculum

The social studies curriculum provides a wealth of interesting topics that can be developed into school library programs. As even the subject area name implies, social studies lends itself to experiential inter-active learning. Therefore, library media specialists frequently create programs relating to the community, citizenship, history, cultures, and geographic regions.

Content that helps students understand their community is essential in the primary grades. For example, many library media specialists feature presentations by the fire department, law enforcement agency, or other community service organizations. Besides fascinating young patrons with details of their work and the uniforms they wear, these visitors often provide brochures and pamphlets that the children can take home. For older students, consider inviting city and state officials such as the local mayor, a state legislator, or a judge.

The world can come to life for elementary students through library events ranging from a single guest speaker to an entire multicultural fair. Parents can share their travel adventures from a recent vacation. Guests from foreign countries can introduce students to aspects of their native culture. In either case, videos and multimedia serve as ideal program support.

Multicultural fairs that highlight the various ethnic groups represented in the school are entertaining, enlightening, and meaningful. Students and teachers enjoy learning unique customs, viewing authentic costumes, and tasting foods from around the world. By hosting such events the library media specialist can certainly strengthen his or her partnership with the social studies teachers. The events also provide excellent PR for the library media center.

Science Curriculum

Science is another content area rife with program opportunities. Because animals hold such a fascination for children, they often serve as perfect subjects for science-related programs. Domestic, wild, or endangered animals, different species, individual breeds, or animals unique to certain regions, climates, or environments can all serve to inspire program ideas.

Beyond the endless possibilities within the animal kingdom are topics related to plants, astronomy, weather, anatomy, and oceanography. Every geographic area has resources that can stimulate ideas for dynamic programs. Naturally, the location of your school can inspire a program idea relevant to students. Coastal towns lend themselves to aquatic themes. Cities like Houston and Orlando can capitalize on NASA's generous offerings in the field of space exploration. Local weather stations of any region can provide support about climate and natural disasters.

Human resources also abound in this curriculum area. At one media center, a permanent display with photographs of famous scientists evolved into a recurring program in which guest scientists, researchers, and doctors visited the school library media center several times each year to make presentations.

Math Curriculum

At one time, media specialists struggled to incorporate math into their curriculum. Thanks to programming, math offers media specialists much more program material. Guest speakers including space engineers, architects, and pilots are tremendously popular with young patrons. Any number of fun contexts can be used to teach math concepts, including setting up a mini-mall where students must add, subtract, and use fractions to purchase items and spend their allotment of play money most economically.

One media specialist, Joann Gerald, used her own love of shopping to create an ongoing learning center where students order "wish list items" from department store catalogs, and then calculate the amount of the order, including taxes and shipping costs. As this example indicates, integrating mathematics principles is often easier in programs that teach real-life skills..

Provide Support and Enrichment
Beyond Core Curriculum

When planning programs, media specialists should remember that using the media center requires skills that students must master to be effective learners. Library instruction itself can most appropriately be highlighted through a library media center program. Searching the Internet, using indexes, or finding resources through the electronic catalog are among the most essential tasks that enhance students' use of the facility. Once the media specialist has targeted a program on a particular area of study, teachers can extend the skill into their classrooms.

Students in special education courses or gifted programs present unique opportunities for programming. Nearly any program can be modified to fit the needs of special populations. Even more important, programs designed to meet these groups' unique talents or needs offer further creative opportunities for media specialists, as well as a more expansive outreach to all members of the student body.

The area of fine arts offers a wealth of programming ideas. Events related to art, music, and drama are worthwhile and tremendously popular with students. Young children are exposed to the work of actors, musicians, or artists daily through the various entertainment media, so inviting a local representative of any of those crafts provides an excellent opportunity for students to discover what creative efforts go into the development and production of a play, CD, or telecast. Programs that focus on displaying student art highlight the artist and decorate the school library media center. (see Photo 1.2)

Photo 1.2. Displays of student art provide an opportunity to share creative projects and to add to the welcoming atmosphere in Julie Hardegree's attractive school library media center. (*Edward White Elementary School, El Lago, Texas, Clear Creek Independent School District*)

As demand for multicultural studies increases, school library media center programs can help fulfill the school's need to cover the material. Again, the media specialist has endless venues through which multiculturalism can be presented. From elaborate fairs, to learning centers, to monthly acknowledgments of different cultures with a simple but attractive bulletin board and accompanying book display, the forum for presenting such material is far-reaching.

Technology is a natural forum for school library media center programs. In such a rapidly evolving discipline, a media specialist could not possibly run out of ideas for offering technology training. With their passion for computers rivaled by little else, students are eager to learn new programs, surf the Internet, and develop the skills to create and design using electronic media.

Provide Personal Enrichment

Programs in the school library media center often focus on the personal interests of students in various grades. By using the knowledge of children's reading and personal interests, media specialists can customize programs to address student interests directly. Where can they find information concerning children's interests? Library circulation statistics and the results of reading interest surveys can provide major clues. Although some general topics of interest remain relatively constant for most age groups, taking a personal inventory of students' likes and dislikes can provide some stark surprises. Often some of the most unique, and unpredictable, topics will become popular among certain groups. From year to year, and sometimes even more frequently, tastes can shift, and entirely new topics will become surefire program ideas for a particular group. Interest surveys keep the media specialist abreast of new trends that will pique student curiosity.

Offering programs on topics that students are intrinsically motivated to learn more about promotes the love of reading. For example, students with a passion for skating may rarely set foot in a school library media center until they hear that a program on the topic is forthcoming. Once they discover that books on skating are available, they may eagerly return to the school library media center for more.

Provide Professional Development
for Teachers

Principals are often pleased when the school library media specialist coordinates professional growth sessions for faculty. In some districts, this is even a requirement. What might first appear merely as an added responsibility is really an outstanding opportunity with long-term professional benefits. Such programs give media specialists the chance to share valuable information while simultaneously establishing and perpetuating a good rapport with their colleagues.

Like programs for students, professional presentations invite ingenuity and creativity. Media specialists need only decide their favorite job activities and develop a program around one of them. PowerPoint experts and Internet explorers are in great demand. New computer programs need introductory demonstrations. Because some online library resources also include classroom access, most teachers would relish learning about resources available in their own room. In addition to demonstrating new programs, teaching new technology and introducing faculty to professional journals make excellent program topics. Sharing with faculty members the selection aids available in the school library media center is invaluable. Whatever the topic, programs for colleagues are effective for three reasons. First, they help the faculty become better teachers. Second, they promote the media center and its media specialist. Finally, they allow media specialists to use their inservice time much more productively. Model programs and various ideas for preparing a professional development program are provided in Chapter 8.

BENEFITS OF PROGRAMMING

Media specialists who integrate special programs into their daily routine will enjoy many benefits and rewards. Such programs offer opportunities to highlight the school library media center as well as the media center staff. At the same time, programming increases use of the library media center, provides classroom support, broadens personal interests, encourages the development of lifelong learners, and provides excellent opportunities for PR.

Highlights the Media Center

By attending programs, students come to view the school library media center as more than a book repository. They become more comfortable there and begin to understand all that the media specialist has to offer. They begin to appreciate that the school library media center is a multifaceted information center filled with attractive displays, interesting learning centers, and unending resources, in both hard copy and electronic formats. Especially for students who rarely frequent a library media center, an exciting, meaningful program can turn them on to learning. Consider providing students and faculty with a tour of the school library media center at the beginning of each school year. Perhaps the tour could be videotaped and shared with anyone who was unable to take part.

Highlights the Media Specialist

Some students do not even know the media specialist; others, unfortunately, think of media specialists only as stereotypically sour dictators who scowl from behind the circulation desk, checking out books and pointing to the "Quiet Please" sign. Offering a program will make such students aware not just that media specialists exist, but also that they are helpful student advocates. To introduce himself to students, one creative media specialist enlarged a photograph of himself and attached a brief biography, including such facts as his favorite books, foods, and movies. A media specialist may choose to share a list of her daily work activities to familiarize students with her job. Students love these personal touches, through which they come to know their media specialist.

Sadly, many administrators also harbor negative stereotypes of the media specialist. A dynamic program can shatter their inaccurate assumptions as well. Programs make media specialists more visible to the student body, the faculty, and, directly or indirectly, the community. Their positive impact promotes the school and reflects well on the principal. As anyone will testify, there is no happier employee than one who helps the boss look good.

Increases School Library Media Center Usage

Following a successful school library media center program, book and media circulation increases markedly. Already impressed by the positive impact the program has made on the school, the principal can also look at subsequent circulation data when completing the media specialist's professional evaluation. When the day comes (and I have never known a media specialist who does not reach that day often) to convince principals of the need for more funds for books, materials, or programs, the data also serve to justify that need.

I can still recall the year that my wish list included a set of encyclopedias on marine life. Following a successful program presented by my guest speaker, a marine biologist, I informed my principal of the increased use of the school library media center on the topic of marine life. Yes, funds somehow became available for me to purchase the new encyclopedia set.

Provides Classroom Support and Enrichment

Programs sponsored by the school library media center are often directly related to what is going on in the classroom. They can act as springboards for units that teachers are introducing, or, as is more often the case, can extend or complete units that had to be cut short to move on to another instructional objective. Either way, programs allow the media specialist to work cooperatively with faculty members to lighten their workload or enhance their effectiveness through extension or repetition. One language arts teacher relishes the school library media center's support of the regular classroom: "Each year I assign my fifth-graders a picture book author such as Maurice Sendak or James Marshall to research. I also require them to read at least two books by the author/illustrator, and to read one of the books aloud and share information about the author with primary children. For this project we depend enormously on the school library media center and our media specialist's support. My fifth-graders love the assignment and enjoy using the resources that the media specialist recommends."

Increased faculty involvement in the school library media center means greater support for the media center. The more teachers bring their classes to the media center, the more vital the facility and the specialist's role in the school, become. Perhaps more dramatically than through any other means, programs establish or cement the partnership between media specialist and teacher.

Broadens Student and Teacher Interests

The revelations of children never cease to astonish. Their excitement is contagious. Priceless are the expressions of a child awed by the sleight of hand of a magician, delighted by an expressive reading from an author, impressed by an artist's talents, or astounded by the discovery that some people actually make a living cooking. Such irreplaceable moments that are the cornerstone of why teachers love to teach are found less frequently in the day-to-day activities of media specialists. But they abound during effective programs.

Equally profound is the response of teachers who discover that they have an ally working in the library media center. Isolated in their classrooms and perpetually inundated with new state and district demands that overwhelm, they relish the knowledge that their heavy load is being shared by a colleague with inventive approaches that add depth and dimension to students' learning. The more that media specialists work with teachers, the more they come to know their needs, and even their personal interests. Acknowledging their individual talents and hobbies is helpful for creating programs and for affirming them as valued co-workers.

Encourages the Development of Lifelong Readers

A major goal of elementary teachers and media specialists is to develop lifelong readers and learners. By providing positive experiences both with books and educational activities through special programs, specialists encourage lifelong learning whereby the students will want to continue reading and learning, even after completing school. Taking the responsibility for one's own personal and professional growth is an ultimate goal that may be reached by showing students during the elementary years that learning is a joy. Fun-filled events in the school library media center, such as storytelling, author visits, and book fairs, encourage positive attitudes toward reading and learning.

Establishes Good Public Relations

Positive responses about school library media center programs from teachers, parents, and students usually filter back to the principal. In some cases, however, it may be up to the media specialist to share this feedback with the principal. Normally, it will be received enthusiastically because any positive news about the school also reflects well on the administration. More personally, it offers an opportunity for the media specialist to be recognized and also to be heard when voicing concerns or making budgetary requests.

Beyond the PR benefits of making a good impression on faculty, administration, and parents, a strong program can also promote the school library media center in the community at large. Inviting local business persons to present at a program serves various purposes:

- It educates students about careers.
- It familiarizes students with the businesses that are the heart of their community.
- It creates a necessary link between the schools and businesses of an area.
- It enables companies to fulfill their community service obligations.
- It unites schools, businesses, and parents in a cooperative effort to help children.

Information on locating and integrating community resources into your school library media center programs is in Chapter 4.

Even those programs that do not draw community members into the school library media center can reach out to them. In advance of a program, media specialists should advertise it in the school and local newspapers, either to invite parents to attend or merely to inform them when the event will transpire. Inviting the local newspaper's photographer to come by that day to take pictures of students attending the event will give the media center a high profile in the community and offer some children the exciting opportunity to appear in the newspaper. Chapter 3 provides effective tips by practicing media specialists on advertising programs.

PROGRAM PARAMETERS

The scope of a school library media center program can be as narrow or as broad as the media specialist sees fit. Whether dictated by student needs, curriculum demands, or the media specialist's own preferences, a full range of parameters for planning a program is available.

Individually Planned Programs

For those media specialists who like the autonomy of working on projects alone, planning and executing a program independently can be most satisfying. Although the parameters for such programs are limited by the media specialist's time, energy, and motivation, they nonetheless have the benefit of being very personally rewarding for media specialists who know they alone have affected students through their efforts.

Joint or Cooperative Programs

No longer an island distinguished from the rest of the school, the media center is instead immersed in every element of the school. The major link between the media center and the classes, of course, is the relationship between the media specialist and the teachers. Thanks to the cooperative approach, media specialists have an entire faculty from which to draw program co-creators. Even more important, the responsibility of a program's success, as well as the work itself, is not shouldered by the media specialist alone. Instead, the media specialist can facilitate the program while inviting various colleagues to use their expertise to develop and prepare the program. With the media specialist as producer and faculty members as both directors and stars, numerous talents combine to create a dynamic, multifaceted event.

Parent and Community Programs

Ideas for developing programs abound throughout the community. Timing programs to coincide with local events often creates long-lasting, thriving bonds between the city or town and media center. Media specialists who contribute their expertise to such events through programs demonstrate support of their community that is likely to be reciprocated by parents who respond to requests for volunteer help.

Parents involved in the special event are often surprised to discover all the advantages of an exciting, active school library media center. While helping in the program, they will likely find many tasks beyond processing books that are interesting and for which they have a special aptitude. Media specialists who have grown weary of making displays can find their school library media center revived by a creative volunteer. Students can benefit from a new voice reading to them or a new set of hands helping them with mastering the computer keyboard. Some parents who initially plan to pass through the media center doors only once for that single program event may be inspired to extend their stay and sign up for a regular volunteer position when they discover the many skills needed to run a school library media center successfully. Tips concerning the recruitment of parent volunteers are discussed in Chapter 5.

THE PUBLIC LIBRARY CONNECTION

To help public librarians see how information in this book can support them as well, we have included this section in Chapter 1 only. Although the context in which they work is different from that of a school library media specialist, the goals and demands of their job are very similar. Especially regarding the Internet resources in Chapter 6 and the sample programs in Chapter 8, public librarians can use the information throughout the entire book by modifying any suggestions and ideas to fit their own professional objectives.

Purpose

Although the age range of a public library's patrons is much broader than that in a school, the needs of public librarians' young patrons parallel those of the school library media center's patrons. Elementary age children must be taught to foster a love of reading if they are to be lifelong learners. To break through the restraints of children thinking that learning only takes place in school, the public librarian can offer programs that go beyond the curriculum demands that may limit school library media specialists. A media specialist may have time only occasionally to offer special interest programs, but public librarians can do so regularly. Besides endearing young patrons to the facility and its staff by addressing their interests, the public librarian is subtly conveying to them that learning is fun, and it takes place everywhere.

Benefits

Offering programs invites children into the public library. The more active the library, the more the librarian is serving the community. Students benefit from a more personalized and hands-on connection to their local library media center. Additionally, programming puts librarians in control of their community involvement. Whereas some libraries have extraneous responsibilities demanded of them (like accommodating voters on election day), a planned program allows them to invite patrons into the library for events they deem relevant to their needs, concerns, and interests. Like a school library media center, a public library media center must overcome limiting ideas of being a book repository. The public librarian can change those misconceptions into positive new impressions through programming.

Parameters

Fortunately, through programs the librarian and his or her staff need not shoulder the responsibility of accommodating young patrons alone. Using local resources, both human and material, is an excellent way to involve the community in the public library.

Not surprisingly, the connection between the public library media center and the schools is a strong lifeline for any community. Knowing that the district's philosophies back both the school and public facilities will help public librarians decide what programs to offer and discern how their unique position of being within the community but not bound by school restrictions can enhance the learning of all children. Communication with school media specialists and teachers can keep public librarians informed of school activities and curriculum. Such knowledge will certainly help when they sit down with their staff to plan events for youngsters.

Even better, public librarians can find their volunteer base through schools. Very often the parents and community members who have participated in school-related programs do not know that their talents are also valuable to the public librarian. When asked, they begin to appreciate the link between the local schools and the community library. Once they have made that discovery, the public librarian can then help them take part in shaping the lives of their children through programs in his or her own facility.

CONCLUSION

In either context, public or school, programs bring libraries and media centers to life. Best of all, their potential is limitless. Whether structuring events around their own natural talents, the interests of students, or curriculum demands, school library media specialists have free reign over what their program offers, how it unfolds, and who it reaches. In a profession that seems to be dictated more and more by administrative and legislative demands, media specialists have a vibrant outlet for exercising their creativity and keeping alive the idea that the school library media center is the heart of the school.

Chapter 2

Initial Stages of Program Planning

Developing and presenting a successful program requires several stages. To illustrate, Sue Wiley, an elementary school library media specialist in Texas, offers the following example of how she planned, presented, and assessed her special event. The italicized scenario that continues throughout Chapter 7 covers only one multifaceted program; however, it serves as a general template for the stages of library programming that can be adapted easily to fit the needs and preferences of most library media specialists. An outline of Sue Wiley's complete program is in Appendix B.

I was desperate to revitalize student interest in my school library media center. Simply continuing the practices of the former library media specialist wasn't working, for the school or for me. Student interest in the media center was dismal, and, not surprisingly, their scholastic performance was generally horrendous. Despite good evaluations from my principal, I was disappointed in my performance as well. Working to exhaustion while making no apparent impact on kids was not what I anticipated when I prepared to enter this profession.

After brainstorming many possibilities, I decided that sponsoring a special program in the school library media center was the best way to generate some excitement in children. To my surprise, few professional resources even addressed the topic. "Flying solo," I determined for myself what would work. First, for my program to be good, I needed a strong focus. At that point, I was certain of only one fact: I had to choose a topic that would attract students and faculty. If I picked a good one, I could at the same time gain publicity for the school. That became my three-part goal. If I achieved it, I was sure I could change how the students, faculty, community, and even I felt about my school library media center.

Instead of feeling lost, I was exhilarated by the limitless prospects. Ideas stirred in my head constantly. As I drove to school each day, possibilities flooded my mind. I would simply jot down ideas and keep searching. At lunch, I started paying close attention to teachers' comments to discover what issues piqued their interest. In the media center, I made mental notes of what the students were most consistently requesting to read. Even lunch duty offered me new opportunities as I eavesdropped on conversations to hear what school-related topics kids talked about beyond the classroom.

For a few weeks I played with ideas to see which had the most potential. Once I narrowed them down to a handful of possibilities, I picked three that I thought would be the most fun to do.

Though I wanted to jump right in and start working on one of them, I realized that gaining teacher support could make or break my program. If teachers were lukewarm about the program, their attitude would rub off on students. Even worse, it would make scheduling the program a nightmare.

So instead of telling the teachers what I was doing after the fact, I brought them into the planning stage. During a weekly fourth-grade curriculum meeting, I asked teachers for input about my three topics: sports, space exploration, and rodeos. As they discussed the possibilities of each, I took notes. Doing so not only gave me new ideas, but it also reinforced my suggestion that I would design a program that they wanted and their students needed. In that one meeting, I got my topic and found a network of supporters who eventually helped kids get enthusiastic about the program.

The teachers agreed that rodeos offered the most exciting possibilities that could be tied in with the rodeo held each year in nearby Houston. Many of our students were already interested in rodeos. The topic could definitely be linked to the fourth-grade social studies unit on Texas. One reason I suggested the idea was because I already had access to many resources related to the topic in my media center and from the district teacher center. I also knew that the Houston Livestock Show and Rodeo organization would have plenty of available resource people and free promotional material that I could use.

As an added bonus, one teacher pointed out that the rodeo theme could also be tied to art and music. The rodeo sponsored a student "Rodeo Art" contest that our school district participated in every year. With the help and advice of the art teacher, I could integrate this contest into my program. I could also incorporate "old cowboy songs," some of which I already had in my Texas folklore collection. Through art and music, I could provide cultural enrichment and academic support for students.

After that grade-level meeting, so many ideas raced through my head that the real challenge became picking which elements to keep in the program. Once I made those decisions, I could move to the next planning stage: choosing which program formats, such as media, special exhibits, learning centers, and guest speakers, would work best in my program.

Sue Wiley's enthusiasm illustrates how exciting ideas are generated when a creative media specialist makes the commitment to develop a program for the school library media center. Executing a successful program requires media specialists to use one innate talent that draws most of them to the profession in the first place: dynamic organizational skills. Other professionals might feel unprepared to tackle the earliest stages of program planning, but most media specialists find that planning program events is similar to their daily responsibilities of planning lessons and activities that support the curriculum. Although it is sometimes challenging to find time to include programming in a busy teaching schedule, the rewards for the library media specialist, the students, and, consequently the entire school, make it worthwhile.

Paramount to the success of any program is the initial planning stage. Generating ideas will flow naturally from patrons' needs and interests, but useful examples and tips throughout this chapter will provide a direct path toward achieving program goals.

CHOOSING A THEME AND GATHERING IDEAS

The first and most important step in the programming process is choosing a topic that will interest students and faculty and that can be presented effectively in the space available. Fortunately, program ideas exist everywhere. Initial observations and brainstorming will generate abundant possibilities. The resulting extensive list can easily be narrowed down when factoring in two requirements for a successful program: It should be easy to develop, and there should be a plethora of resources readily available.

Many media specialists begin generating ideas alone; however, brainstorming with teachers, students, and other media specialists is usually faster and more fruitful. If a target audience, for example, fourth-graders, is established before the idea stage, then brainstorming with the fourth-grade teachers, or with a student committee who represents them, will expedite the planning process even more. Although curriculum-based programs are important, programs that solely address student interests are every bit as valid. Determine a purpose for the program, and let each stage support that plan. From enhancing core learning to encouraging reading with fun activities, programs are as varied as the audiences they serve.

Many program ideas result from direct exploration, but others can develop unexpectedly. A passing comment from a student or teacher about a topic of interest or a curriculum area can trigger a great program concept. Sometimes ideas come from curriculum topics or special projects already being highlighted in the classroom. Other ideas may come from workshops, seminars, or conferences. Some of the most interesting themes are derived from what is happening in the community or even from timely issues covered in the newspaper.

When choosing a theme and developing ideas for the upcoming program, consider using a combination of suggestions by faculty and other media specialists, student interests, curriculum needs, professional development activities, and community happenings.

Faculty Suggestions

It's always wise to solicit input from teachers. The essential partnership between media specialists and faculty will be strengthened by regular, meaningful communication. Often through conversations with faculty, media specialists discover untapped program ideas of great promise. Teachers with extensive and current content area knowledge can inspire great program ideas. Placing a suggestion box in the teachers' lounge or professional library can encourage teachers to offer recommendations for programs (see Figure 2.1). Some suggestions by faculty can be predictable, such as author visits, or visits by local firefighters or police officers, or special historical events like Pioneer Day, but frequently a teacher may spark an original idea that excites the entire faculty. For example, because so few students at an inner city school in Chicago had the opportunity to travel, one fifth-grade teacher suggested a program, "Travel Across the United States," as an enrichment activity. In collaboration with fifth-grade teachers, the media specialist developed a tremendously successful month-long program in the school library media center. Each week the fifth-graders traveled vicariously to famous tourist attractions such as the Alamo, Yellowstone National Park, and the Grand Canyon. Guest speakers acted as tour guides, showing multimedia presentations that they created and sharing relevant historical and geographical facts provided by the media specialist.

Beyond the one-on-one interactions that are part of a media specialist's weekly routine, involvement in grade-level meetings and on curriculum committees can provide a wealth of ideas for school library media center programs. In whatever context, all written or oral suggestions from teachers should be seriously considered and officially recorded in some manner. Ideas with the potential to meet student needs and fit the media center's schedule and budget restraints should then be explored in depth with the faculty member. As mentioned previously, determine if resources on the topic are already available. While brainstorming with the colleague, inquire whether he or she, or the department, has more resources on hand, and if he or she has contacts who can provide more. Pinpoint as many concrete ideas as possible and continue the dialogue until the initial suggestion takes shape as a manageable, worthwhile program concept. Pursued thoroughly, a single brainstorming session often provides the information from which the entire school library media center program can be developed. Just as important, that single meeting usually introduces other program ideas that can be explored in the future.

SUGGESTION FORM

_____ We need more books on the following topics:

_____

_____

_____

_____ Please order the following titles(s) for our school library media center:

_____

_____

_____

_____ We need more books written by the following author(s):

_____

_____

_____

_____ I would enjoy attending a program in the school library media center about the following topic(s):

_____

_____

_____

_____

_____

Figure 2.1. Teacher/student suggestion form.

Other Media Specialists

Generating ideas with other media specialists in a district can prove especially fruitful. Quite likely, colleagues can share programming successes to emulate and point out mistakes to avoid. In most districts, other media specialists are happy to share resources that would enhance a program. Brainstorming with fellow media specialists often results in collaborative events that benefit all. For example, media specialists in one school district pooled their resources for an extended author visit from children's poet Jack Prelutsky. Media specialists from the various schools collaborated in the program planning, shared promotional ideas and activities, developed a schedule by which Prelutsky visited each elementary school during the week, and planned a districtwide reception to honor him. By working together, the media specialists were able to afford and execute a plan that was exciting, meaningful, and memorable for all their students.

Student Interests

Just as interests play an important role in book selection, they can also provide clues to help media specialists select topics for events sponsored by the library media center. The magnetic appeal of recreational and personal interests often brings students naturally into the learning process. What they are curious about, they will learn about. How can a media specialist determine what will draw students into the school library media center? Query the target audience. Simple observation or direct feedback from current students can apprise program planners of current trends sure to draw patrons. Trends can be volatile, so it is safe and wise to continue focusing on topics in which children show a more permanent interest and continue to enjoy over the years, such as animals, sports, and art.

Both current fads and permanent interests are important considerations when selecting a program theme. Programs related to the more stable areas of interest can be repeated and become more refined each time they are presented. For example, an energetic media specialist in New England focuses on fascinating hobbies for an annual program sponsored by the school library media center. Last year she featured two parents recognized in the community for their hobbies. A gardening enthusiast and a cook visited the school library media center to share their knowledge with fourth-graders. For months following the presentations, excited students checked out gardening books and cookbooks that had previously stood dormant on the shelves.

When determining a program theme, consider the geographical area in which the students live. For example, Sue Wiley lives near Houston, which sponsors one of the largest livestock shows and rodeos in the world. Calf roping and barrel racing are sports topics relevant to Texas students, but they would mean little to young people in some other areas. A school in Fort Lauderdale might generate excitement by focusing on sailing or surfing, and in Denver a program on snow skiing would interest students. Clearly, geographic location can determine the relevance, and success, of some program ideas.

Just as students offer great suggestions for books to order, they also can suggest possible program topics that they would enjoy. Placing a suggestion form and box in a prominent place in the school library media center invites students to offer suggestions as the need arises. It also enables media specialists to read, collect, and consider the feedback when they have time to do so. Feedback gathered over time also allows the media specialist to select program topics based on frequent requests that reflect the personal interests of students.

Another way to identify student interests is to ask each teacher to have students complete a reading interest survey at the beginning of the school year. (see Figure 2.2, page 30) The major purpose of such a survey is to determine children's reading interests so that teachers and media specialists can match children with the appropriate books. The survey is also a dynamic tool for program development. Knowing students' personal interests enables media specialists to offer programs that appeal to students at specific grade levels. Even better, having the information at the beginning of the school year allows media specialists to consider program ideas and gather further data long before program planning begins.

Curriculum Needs

To match program topics with required learning goals, media specialists should first be familiar with the school curriculum. Textbooks and curriculum guides that contain all of the core information serve as excellent starting points. At every grade level, students study topics and learn skills that build on previous knowledge. Noting this scope and sequence is essential to matching program content to the appropriate audience.

Within the curriculum, program opportunities abound. For example, if you discover that first-graders study "community helpers" in the early fall, do more than order current resources on the topic. Invite a firefighter or a police officer to campus as a guest speaker for a program. One media specialist, Paul Richards, extended a program beyond the walls of his school library media center by inviting students to visit the firetruck on display in the parking lot, then attend a presentation on fire safety in the school media center. With knowledge of curriculum, Paul created an exciting and effective learning experience that required only ingenuity and a little extra preparation.

STUDENT INTEREST SURVEY

Grade: _____   Sex: ___ M ___ F

What is your favorite book? _____

What is your favorite hobby?_____ Sport? _____

What are your favorite subjects at school? _____

What do you do for entertainment at home? _____

What types of books do you enjoy reading?

      ___ picture books   ___ biographies
      ___ animals   ___ fantasy
      ___ historical fiction   ___ poetry
      ___ science   ___ mystery
      ___ folk literature   ___ realistic fiction
      ___ humorous stories   ___ adventure stories
      ___ science fiction   ___ information books

If you checked information books, what kind of information books do you like?

_____

_____

_____

What types of library programs would you enjoy attending?

      ___ animals   ___ art
      ___ careers   ___ computers
      ___ cooking   ___ crafts
      ___ cultures   ___ dance
      ___ hobbies   ___ travel
      ___ sports   ___ music

Other: _____

_____

Figure 2.2. Student interest survey.

Familiarity with the curriculum comes from serving on curriculum committees and attending grade-level meetings. Although many administrators already include the media specialist in planning meetings, others may have to be reminded how integral the library media specialist is to the school. Having extensive knowledge of the existing policies and curriculum proves a credible argument for inclusion. Also, sharing information about the outstanding resources in the media center suggests that, appropriately, the library media center is a key element in a successful school.

Whatever persuasion works, be sure to become part of the school's decision-making team. The meetings will provide relevant information about curricular needs and classroom activities that can be used when ordering materials. At the same time, knowledge gleaned at the meetings provides the perfect background for developing program ideas. In the end, everyone benefits from the collaborative effort. The curriculum is enriched and supported, brainstorming sessions are more fruitful, resource circulation increases, and student learning is enhanced because knowledge is presented in a more interesting way.

Professional Development Activities

Attending conferences, workshops, and courses in the school district as well as at universities can enhance program development. By maintaining a mindset of looking for ideas or special topics at such events, media specialists soon discover that program ideas arise everywhere. A media specialist in Colorado reported that her recent program for faculty, "Children's Book Choices," resulted from her attendance at the state reading conference.

Professional journals and teacher magazines are excellent sources for event ideas. Simply reading about a program that worked for someone else may ignite a spark for designing a similar program or developing a more elaborate one on the same topic.

A visit to the professional collection at the district or school level can inspire possibilities for program themes as well as offer a wealth of resources that can be used in planning the event. For example, during the planning stage Sue Wiley visited the district teacher center to refine her programming topic on rodeos and to determine the variety of resources available for the program. In addition to book resources, she discovered a video produced by the Houston Livestock Show and Rodeo that traced its impressive history.

Community Happenings

Local events often trigger theme ideas for media specialists who are searching for exciting programs. Each community enjoys a wealth of special holidays, festivals, fairs, and cultural activities that can provide topics for school library media center programs. Community organizations, universities, bookstores, and museums often highlight special programs and can serve as excellent sources of program ideas. Knowledge of the dates and speakers involved in the activities is essential for tying programs to community events. In fact, Sue Wiley's rodeo concept evolved partly from the fact that a rodeo was a major "happening" in her community each year. Another program sponsored by the library media center evolved because a perceptive media specialist imagined how well the local "Balloon Fest" could translate into a fun-filled school library media center event. Media specialists who work where such events take place could easily use this concept. Even those who do not have such an event to tie into can teach students about related topics such as the history of aviation and transportation or science concepts on gravity and gases. Newspapers frequently document world record enthusiasts trying to span the globe in a balloon. Helping students follow a tracking chart during such journeys is a great geography tool and a fun activity. Ideas, approaches, and formats for any topic are endless.

Besides events, special holidays make excellent program topics. Bored with the usual Thanksgiving, Christmas, and Valentine themes? Use programs to help students learn about elections or veterans in November, Martin Luther King Jr. in January, and Mexico's traditions and history on Cinco de Mayo.

Looking for topics with more immediacy for students? Check out upcoming local events. When are they going to happen? Who is involved? Answers to these questions are rife with program possibilities. Keep up with the local newspaper, magazines, radio, and television where program ideas abound. Seeking a more direct approach? Call the local Chamber of Commerce and request the community calendar of events, which lists information about what is going on locally. Additionally, contacting the organizer of a community event can open the door to carrying over the event to the library media center. Such contacts also result in positive publicity for the library media center as well as the school.

After contacting her Chamber of Commerce, media specialist Fran Cyburt found that an antique car collection would be in the city in April. Immediately, she began planning a related event of her own to occur simultaneously with the city's. The program focused on using the school library media center's locked display case to display a student's collection of model antique cars. Books on the topic and a poster advertising the car show were also displayed near the case. The community's excitement about the local antique car show was felt in the school library media center as students eagerly visited the miniature collection of antique cars. Best of all, Austin, the student who shared his model cars with the school, was not only recognized by the media specialist for his generosity but also gained new respect from classmates who knew little about him before the event.

The vast resources in the community, including special events, people, places, and things, are invaluable support for specialists, both when determining themes as well as during the later stages of program development. Chapter 4 lists a wealth of community resources that can be used to develop program ideas and gather resources.

DEVELOPING A SPECIFIC PLAN

To mold a general idea into a more concrete, workable plan, answer the following questions:

- What are my general goals for the program?

- Who will this topic interest? (grade, age, gender)

- What format (displays, centers, speakers) will I use for this program?

- Where will I find available resources on the topic?

- When is the best date and time to offer the program?

- What will the logistics of carrying out this program involve?

Setting Goals

With the theme established and general program ideas outlined, it is time to develop clear goals. Before starting, have the end in mind. List the precise purposes for the program. What final benefits will participants derive from the program? In developing the goals, relate every one either to curriculum or to the personal interests of the students and faculty. Programs based on such goals are unquestionably relevant to participants in the context of the school. Formally writing the goals is essential to the planning process because it establishes a clear focus that becomes the core of the entire program.

The best programs take advantage of a combination of approaches. For example, Sue Wiley's model program (shared in Appendix B) indicates that she drew upon a variety of sources. Through brainstorming and discussions with faculty, Sue was able to select a relevant and riveting topic. Her knowledge of curriculum, student interests, professional resources, and community events proved essential in generating specific ideas for program development. Now she was ready to move on to the next stage: clarifying the goals for her program, "Rodeos and Cowboys: Today and Yesterday."

After getting plenty of input from my faculty, I thought I was ready to plan a program. But jumping right in without more of a plan made me realize that I had no sense of direction. I knew I needed a new, and clearer strategy. So I added a step, this time deciding on some specific goals. So, after a little refining, I came up with these:

- *To familiarize students with materials that focus on cowboys and rodeos.*

- *To share information with students about rodeos and cowboys of today and our past.*

- *To share with students the activities that go on behind the scenes at a rodeo.*

- *To tie school activities to a major community event.*

Considering the Audience

When developing programs for students, match the theme to the age, interests, and gender of the audience. Some programs may also require consideration of such factors as the maturity of the students and their fine motor skills. Although occasionally planning a program for all students in the school can be appropriate, targeting a specific segment of the population, such as gifted and talented students, first-graders, or all primary students, ensures several benefits for the media specialist and the students.

Narrowing the focus allows the media specialist to address the learning needs of a more specific segment of the student population, thereby ensuring a more meaningful learning experience. Additionally, events for smaller populations are easier to schedule. It would be unrealistic to plan huge extravaganzas every month, but media specialists could potentially offer programs on a monthly basis by planning small group events or by choosing from the easy programming ideas in Chapter 8. Grand productions reap outstanding benefits for the media specialist and the school, but they are more manageable and meaningful when offered as unique, and rare, events.

Matching the appropriate audience to the topic is essential. Therefore, once the program topic and presentation plan are secure, consider the following questions regarding the audience:

- Is the topic appropriate for the maturity level of the audience?

- Will the topic pique the audience's interest?

- Are the length and content of the activities appropriate for the audience's maturity level?

- Will the planned activities hold the audience's attention?

- What new knowledge will the audience gain from the program?

Also consider providing programs for faculty or parents. Programs for faculty, such as those shared in Chapter 8, can focus on any number of professional growth topics ranging from technology to reference materials and children's literature. For example, a media specialist in Idaho recently invited faculty to a workshop, "The Top 25 Children's Books," presented by a local children's bookstore. (The books were made available for faculty to purchase at a 15 percent discount.) The program was so well received that faculty requested that it become an annual event.

Parents also appreciate invitations to special events in the school library media center. In one Florida school district, parent attendance is always great for the annual program, "Books Too Good to Miss," which is held in conjunction with the school library media center's book fair in mid-November, prior to the holiday season. Through short booktalks, the media specialist inspires parents to share good books with their children by presenting a 30-minute overview of outstanding new books for children. Not coincidentally, the books that she highlights are readily available at the book fair. This event generates great revenue for the media specialist, who uses her book fair profits to pay for other events that she sponsors in the spring.

No matter what the general target audience, it is usually possible, and often advisable, to narrow the group. To her surprise, Sue Wiley discovered this fact by accident in her program, "Rodeos and Cowboys: Today and Yesterday."

Even with my program goals, I was still hazy about my target audience. I knew the topic was perfect for my fourth-graders. It matched their interests, and I could easily tie the rodeo theme to their social studies curriculum on Texas. On the other hand, it was a topic that appealed to all grade levels and both genders. Since I was going to do the work putting it together anyway, I seriously considered opening it up to the whole school. Luckily, since it was my first major program, I was worried that I might be trying more than I could handle. In the end, I decided to offer the program only to the fourth-grade students. I quickly discovered what a smart choice that was. With a limited target audience, I could meet my list of goals much more reasonably. If the program was successful, I could repeat it annually to fourth-graders so that all students in the school would eventually get to take part.

Determining a Time Frame

In some cases media specialists may wait until they have determined what resources are available; however, most program planners have a sense of the time frame early in the planning process. Some media center programs may cover a brief period of time. For example, some programs may focus on a single speaker for a 30-minute period. Other programs, such as displays or exhibits, may be continued throughout an entire month. When planning the more extravagant events, the time frame can be extended for a long period of time. In fact, one media specialist in Oregon planned a program theme for an entire year in recognition of the 25th anniversary of the elementary school.

Identifying Resources

With clear program goals, a target audience, and a specific time frame, the school library media specialist has only to identify appropriate materials to complete this stage in the planning process. When selecting from the multitude of resources, consider the following factors:

- Age of audience

- Maturity level of audience

- Interest level of audience

- Audience's background knowledge of topic

- Content of material

- Appropriateness of material for a school program

- Appropriateness of material for program format

- Currency of material

- Accessibility of material

- Availability of support materials on topic

Various types of resources can support the media specialist's programming efforts. Community resources, media software, children's literature, professional literature, exhibits, and displays are among the most frequently used resources. Additionally, teacher-made and student-made resources are readily available to enrich media center programs. This particular topic warrants an entire chapter; therefore, Chapter 4 is devoted to the identification of resources. It also provides tips for organizing the resources to support future programs in the media center.

Choosing a Format

With resources to support the goals, it is now time to consider the type of program to develop. The format or program design is often reflected in the amount of time allocated for preparing the programming event(s). This preparation time varies according to the format selected, as programming can range from a simple display to a sophisticated full-day or ongoing event. Each format listed below offers tremendous flexibility. Programs of any type can be as simple or as sophisticated as the media specialist desires. Careful selection of format is an important phase in program development, and format choices are often dependent on audience, amount of facility space, and established goals. Although the simplest programs usually involve a single format like those discussed below, keep in mind that some programs, such as Sue Wiley's event, incorporate several formats to meet the specific program goals.

Exhibits and Displays

Exhibits and displays are the most frequently used form of programming in school library media centers. Surprisingly, however, many media specialists do not realize that this common format is a form of programming. For example, one media specialist indicated in a recent survey that she had not developed a program in her school library media center in years. However, later in a telephone interview she described the children's artwork, such as dioramas, that she routinely displays in her school library media center. Exhibits and displays can be tied to most themes and can focus on the curriculum as well as personal interests. They come in a variety of forms, including

- bulletin boards,
- wall displays,
- mobiles,
- display cases,
- display shelves,
- table exhibits,
- free-standing displays, and
- traveling trunks.

Some media specialists like to feature a different topic in the school library media center each month. This form of programming can be organized in various ways. In many cases the media specialist plans the featured topic and prepares the related exhibit or display.

Programs that feature speakers or media presentations as main events can be supplemented through the use of exhibits or displays before, during, or after the major event. For example, following a program that focused on a guest speaker from Japan, students were invited to browse the table display of books as well as the display case that featured a kimono, a hand-painted fan, chopsticks, and a Japanese tea service.

Because of its simplicity, this format is a favorite of media specialists who have never before developed a school library media program. Display cases, table displays, or bulletin boards to attract patrons to the school library media center are usually the least time-consuming to construct; however, even these simple designs require more program development than simply placing items in a display case or hanging art on a bulletin board. The execution of a successful program results when the media specialist puts time into actually planning the displays around a particular topic, developing goals to go with the display, and taking the time to write labels or explain the exhibits to the students and teachers. The most common displays, such as children's art, focus on aesthetic appeal. More involved displays can be rich in content. Labeling objects with titles and descriptions promotes the enrichment of student vocabulary, provides curriculum-related information, and shares intriguing trivia that can inspire patrons to explore further reading opportunities.

Exhibits and displays are particularly useful for attracting students who would not otherwise want to visit the school library media center. Often, reluctant children who step into the media center to view the

items on display acquire a positive attitude toward the media center and are more likely to return. Who knows? It may even encourage them to check out a book on the topic. The most important benefit is that students realize that school library media centers offer more than books for checkout. (see Photo 2.1)

Photo 2.1. Students enjoy viewing the "habitats" exhibit that supports the school's curriculum. *(George Washington Elementary School, Kingsport, Tennessee, Kingsport City Schools)*

Program development related to an exhibit or display is limited only by the media specialist's motivation and creativity. Information about identifying special exhibits and displays to meet certain thematic needs is provided in Chapter 4.

Because Sue Wiley, like most media specialists, was already comfortable with creating book displays, she recognized the advantages of using the display format for her program. They were easy to use, and she had many books already available in her media center. Therefore, she decided at an early planning stage to include an interesting display of books and other resources in her program plans.

Featured Speakers or Entertainers

School library media center events that focus on various themes can include one or more guest speakers. This format could involve inviting one or several speakers to share information on a single topic of interest to students. At a recent school library media center event in Salt Lake City, for example, an airline pilot visited the media center to chat with fifth-graders about her profession. In a similar but more involved program, a military pilot, a private pilot, and a commercial airline pilot were the featured speakers for grades four and five. Because of the audience size, the three pilots presented to each grade level separately for 20-minute sessions. Students were divided into groups that rotated among the three speakers until every student had heard each presentation.

Programs that feature guest speakers can be planned and carried out in a variety of ways to meet the needs of students and match the teaching styles of guest speakers. Program formats include

- a single speaker presenting the topic to one group,
- a single speaker presenting the topic multiple times,
- multiple speakers presenting their topics to one group,
- multiple speakers presenting their topics at multiple times, and
- multiple speakers presenting their topics in different areas of the facility at the same time on the same topic.

Interest and Learning Centers

Teachers routinely establish interest centers and learning centers in their classrooms to supplement, reinforce, and/or enrich a unit or learning experience on a specific topic. Consider using this form of programming in the school library media center. Like exhibits, these formats can vary from the very simple center idea to the more involved learning experience.

Interest centers and learning centers attract students to the media center while also supporting the school library media center or classroom curriculum. Learning centers can be used to supplement and enrich library skills lessons and extend class curriculum, and they can also provide activities following special programming events such as presentations by guest speakers. A single activity can comprise a learning center, or a learning center can be more elaborately designed to include several activities, supporting posters, instructions, or artwork, and other resources. Placement of activities is open to the media specialist's ingenuity and is limited only by the size of the facility. Center activities should be changed frequently. They work well in individual carrels, on table tops, within divider units, and in any space that offers an opportunity to focus on a specific independent or small group activity. Interest centers also provide enrichment and can be established in various spots in the library media center. They usually include interesting items or objects that stimulate thought and prompt discussion among students. For example, an aquarium in the media center usually inspires children to learn more about fish.

Developing a program around these formats involves more than simply setting them up. Regardless of the program, three simple steps should always be addressed:

1. Select an interesting theme or topic.

2. Carefully define the goals.

3. Carefully select the resources that will be used.

Media specialists who appreciate the educational value of including centers in the school library media center often create unique ways of spotlighting them. As an elementary media specialist, I developed some of my most successful programs around learning centers. For one program, I hung a yellow polka-dotted shoebag on a wall in the school library media center. It magically became a learning center entitled "Shoebag of Treats." In each of 12 separate pockets, I inserted a paperback book and a literature-based activity. Throughout the semester, I routinely changed the activities and books. In another area of the school library media center I engaged youngsters in center activities in six individual "cubby holes" designed from particle board that divided the large rectangular tables in the school library media center. (see Photo 2.2)

Photo 2.2. Students are absorbed in a learning center activity related to media specialist Susan Link's "Book a Trip Around the World" program. *(Colony Bend Elementary, Sugar Land, Texas, Fort Bend Independent School District)*

When identifying stimulating learning center activities, consider topics that will interest students, such as:

- Aviation center
- Detective center
- Computer center
- Career center
- Music center
- Sports center
- Fantasy center

- Farming center
- Art center
- Ecology center
- Interior design center
- Storytelling center
- Crafts center
- Author center

Demonstrations

Demonstrations are usually presented by special guests who are experts in their fields. In some cases, however, students may be invited to the school library media center to view a previously filmed demonstration or a commercial video. A program can involve a single demonstration or multiple demonstrations by different people. For one program in Ohio, a local artist discussed and demonstrated the art of silk screen design during a special school library media center program. Samples of his work were displayed for students to enjoy, and teachers gave students an opportunity to work with silk screen design in the classroom. Because of the success of this program, the media specialist expanded the program during the following year by inviting three different artists to demonstrate their unique art techniques: silk screening, painting with watercolors, and computer graphic designing. For this particular program the media specialist established three different centers (or stations). Small groups of students visited each center, learned about the art technique, viewed the display of art forms, and eagerly took part in hands-on activities planned by each artist.

Demonstrations can be developed around almost any theme, such as

- cooking,
- using computer soft-ware,
- silk screening,
- drawing,
- dancing,

- puzzle solving,
- baking,
- pet grooming,
- scrapbook (or "memory book") designing, or
- Internet communicating.

Media Programs

Commercially produced media materials abound and can be tied to almost any thematic program in the school library media center. Films, recordings, and computer software that focus on children's books and authors, community resources, special holidays, and other topics can enrich school library media center programs. They can also be used as extended classroom experiences. Likewise, media presentations make effective and engaging professional development programs for faculty.

Sue Wiley decided to incorporate a media element into her rodeo program after finding an excellent video resource.

The fourth-grade teachers who convinced me to choose the rodeo theme assured me that I could easily find a number of videos available on the topic. It was in my search that I came upon a video produced by the Houston Livestock Show and Rodeo. With that, I hit the jackpot! Though I didn't immediately know how and when during the program I could use the film, I realized after one viewing that turning my program into a multimedia presentation would raise the quality of my program considerably.

CONCLUSION

The format or design for programs will vary according to special needs, interests, and program goals. The time frame for the program and the creativity of the media specialist dictate whether those goals will best be met by one speaker, one media event, or a combination of several guests and activities. In the case of Sue Wiley, finding a video sparked her creativity and turned a streamlined plan into a multidimensional, major event. With program goals and learning objectives in mind, begin the process of putting together your program. New facets to your program and unexpected resources will inevitably result in refinements to your original plan. Modify as necessary. As the expert, you will know what changes will enhance your program and make it greater than even you originally thought possible.

Chapter 3

Final Stages of Program Planning

As her ideas gelled into a workable plan, Sue Wiley's enthusiasm began breathing new life into her school library media center.

After a month of planning my rodeo program, I was pleasantly stunned by how much this project was already impacting me professionally. Working with teachers and researching my program topic taught me more about curriculum than I ever knew before. I had examined the curriculum guides before, but until I needed to apply the curriculum to my own program goals, it never had as much meaning for me as a media specialist.

In planning "Rodeos and Cowboys," I kept coming up with different formats that I could use with my themes. The more options I discovered, the more enthusiastic and creative I became. Even before I finished preparing the program, I began to see how much better my library would be as a result.

Best of all, I felt that I was really contributing something exceptional to the school. While working with the fourth-grade teachers, I was developing a closer bond with them. I also gained a new appreciation for the creative freedom I enjoyed as a media specialist that I did not have as a teacher. Though I was using the curriculum in my program, I was not tied to it as tightly as they were. With my program, I had the freedom to pick which curriculum goals I wanted to tackle, and then had the freedom to select how and when I would do the work.

That work continued into the final phase of carrying out the logistics of the program.

OUTLINING THE PROGRAM CONTENT

After deciding your theme, goals, audience, time frame, and available resources, determine the specific content for your program. Making this decision now enables you to select only the most relevant resources. With your content and goals in mind, begin your research. Talk to teachers, examine reference materials and professional resources, and explore the burgeoning data available over the Internet. During this stage, ideas will begin to solidify into a concrete program plan. A clear vision invites better communication and allows you to ask the right questions for securing resource persons, businesses, organizations, and potential helpers.

OBTAINING ADMINISTRATIVE APPROVAL

Know the district's policies for granting permission for major programs. What is the chain of command that must be followed? In most cases, it begins with asking the principal for permission concerning any activity that includes inviting guest speakers or renting free-standing exhibits. School districts are often concerned about the specific theme and content of certain programs, particularly those not related to the school curriculum. Obviously, simple curriculum-related programs that focus on centers and table or wall displays can be done without permission. However, even when planning these forms of programs, it is a good idea to keep the principal apprised of all upcoming events. After developing the theme and having a good idea of the content, share programming ideas and goals with the principal. Always let him or her know about major media center events, focusing especially on the positive PR they generate for the school. Follow up any visit by sending a brief memo outlining the discussion and thanking the principal for his or her time and receptivity. Also, invite the principal to every program. Informally ask the principal to visit your library media center for smaller events. When hosting an elaborate program, send a written invitation to your principal. Even if the principal slips in for a brief moment to observe a sliver of a presentation or view a display of children's work, the positive rapport established by including the principal is essential to getting recognition and respect. Over time, even a handful of small programs can make a lasting impression.

Principals are usually pleased when their media specialists take the initiative to develop a special program for the students and teachers in the school. Sometimes the principal is eager to collaborate with the media specialist, which can even result in funding for special programs. The backing of the principal often empowers media specialists to achieve many goals in their school library media centers that would otherwise be much more difficult, or even impossible.

Establishing a good rapport with her principal, Mr. Johnson, paid off for Sue Wiley.

In November I scheduled an appointment with my principal to discuss the possibility of presenting the month-long "Rodeos and Cowboys" program in February. I brought an outline of my program ideas to the meeting. As I discussed the topic, my goals, and the activities that I would include, Mr. Johnson became very enthused. Even before I got to the part about what great PR the program could be for the school, Mr. Johnson suggested I share the event in the district newsletter. He not only gave his enthusiastic approval, but he also gave me the names of some possible resources that came in handy.

SECURING TEACHER SUPPORT

Successful programs need faculty support. Throughout the development stages of program planning, request teacher input for the upcoming event. Their feedback can improve your program markedly. Also, contributing teachers develop a sense of "ownership" and excitement about the event, which can generate schoolwide anticipation for the program. Simple marketing strategies can generate great enthusiasm for the project:

- Share the upcoming program idea with the grade-level faculty involved.

- Encourage grade-level faculty to provide input into the program and extended activities.

- Provide faculty with sample activities related to the program.

- At a faculty meeting, share with the faculty the program theme and plans for the specific target group.

- Inform faculty that program announcements will continue throughout the planning process.

- To avoid resistance from some groups, assure the entire staff that similar programs for their grade levels will be planned in the future.

In general, Sue Wiley was pleased by faculty response to her announcement.

Because some fourth-grade teachers were already helping with my program, I announced our plan so that no other grade levels felt slighted. I shared my news by asking for teachers' help in gathering program resources. Initially, the third-grade teachers were disappointed that this program targeted only fourth-graders, but once I assured them of my intent to repeat the program annually, they were pleased to know that their current students would eventually benefit from our efforts. In the process, I even received some unexpected help. A fifth-grade teacher who owns horses volunteered to contribute items for the table display.

PLANNING THE SPECIFIC DETAILS

Parts of this next phase are often considered the most difficult. Scheduling a time, date, and location for a special event is dependent on many factors, not the least of which is the rigid schedule to which most schools must adhere. When also taking into consideration the scheduling of both human and material resources, the potential for conflicts expands. Fortunately, library media specialists are accustomed to handling multiple responsibilities simultaneously and to working around others' less flexible time constraints. As a result, this stage requires only some extra planning and some creative negotiating.

Select and Verify a Location

After obtaining the principal's approval and support, it is time to decide on the best location for the program. Conveniently, the school library media center is the ideal location for most programs. One primary goal of any program is to publicize the media center. What better way to do this than to invite students into the facility to enjoy a riveting program? By taking part in an activity in the school library media center, patrons let go of stereotypical impressions of a cold, musty chamber of silence run by a sour old stick figure in a moth-eaten sweater and gray bun. Instead, they begin to view media centers as vibrant places filled with interesting materials and activities. Special programs encourage students who rarely frequent the school library media center to return to the center for browsing through materials or viewing displays; checking out a book is not always required.

Although most programs take place in the school library media center, even it can be difficult to schedule. Therefore, when planning an event in the facility, schedule it well in advance. On the other hand, it is possible that the center does not provide the necessary space needed to carry out the program, and only another facility can handle the crowd. Exciting programs such as a visit to the school by a pilot in a hot air balloon have been set on the playground. Others have been presented in special classrooms, on the school patio, or in the auditorium. Events are occasionally scheduled off campus, as in the case of a North Carolina media specialist who organized a program for faculty at the district professional library. Handle off-campus programs as you would a field trip: Secure transportation, complete appropriate permission slips, and adhere to other district rules and policies.

For Sue Wiley, choosing the time and place of her program was helped by having selected a smaller target audience.

> Deciding the WHERE and WHEN of my program was made thousands of times easier, thanks to my limited audience. It never occurred to me to host a program anywhere besides my library media center which, fortunately, is quite spacious. This turned out to be lucky. Because it is large enough to accommodate the whole fourth-grade at once, I was saved the headache of having to organize two separate events and asking the guest speaker to do a presentation twice. Luckily, it could also handle the ancillary programs that I wanted to include in other formats, such as learning centers, exhibits, and the video presentation.

Choose and Confirm a Date and Time

Scheduling an event is often the most difficult job. At the earliest reasonable opportunity, secure a precise date for the program. Reaching that concrete decision, however, requires first selecting several tentative dates and times that might work, then coordinating them with other campus events on the school calendar. Determine two possible dates that do not conflict with other school programs, then investigate the following factors:

- School schedule
- Availability of resource persons
- Availability of faculty
- Availability of support personnel, such as volunteers and aides
- Availability of resource materials that support the presentation

With these restrictions in mind, schedule small programs at least four to six weeks ahead of the program date. Schedule the extravaganzas several months in advance.

Working around the school calendar, and particularly class schedules, can be another major stumbling block in the planning process.

Media specialists and teachers are experienced in working around class, lunch, music, and physical education schedules. Conducting a program for the school will certainly make use of these scheduling skills. To get backing from teachers for the best time and date, it is important to discuss the matter thoroughly with colleagues at grade-level and faculty meetings. Clearly, two major purposes for sponsoring a program are to create positive impressions of the library media center and to improve its effectiveness in the school. What better way to achieve these goals than to strengthen rapport with teachers? Generally, and understandably, they do not appreciate disruptions to their schedule. However, when they have input into the schedule and event, their attitude toward it, and toward the library media center, becomes supportive. This is especially true when the content of the program ties in with their curriculum and thus serves as an extension of their teaching. Without question, teachers' support of the event is essential. To get it, include them in the planning.

Select and Schedule Guest Speakers

What is the best way to identify speakers for special events? The local community is filled with resource possibilities. Chapter 4 includes useful information about locating a guest speaker. Chapter 6 goes a step further and lists numerous Web sites of resources such as businesses, institutions, and authors that can help connect program planners with speakers.

Selecting appropriate speakers is critical for programming. Most important, the resource person must be interesting to a young audience. The content should be interesting and appropriate to the age level of the audience. Thanks to their professional experience, most library media specialists can determine quite a bit about the potential speaker's ability to relate to children even during initial conversations. Professionals who project a presence to which children can relate make vibrant, often entertaining guests for students. The success of this program design depends entirely on the effectiveness of the person selected. Therefore, know the intended speaker.

Like most people, I have attended some ineffective programs because the guest speaker could not relate to the audience. The topic may have been relevant, the material well organized and useful, but the speaker simply could not connect with those in attendance. Among adults, that can be frustrating. With children, it can be disastrous. Even some speakers with solid professional credentials, an impressive body of knowledge, and plenty of speaking experience may not be the best choice for elementary youngsters. Consequently, prior to the program determine whether the resource person is a good match for your patrons.

How can a library media specialist make that decision with confidence? There are no guarantees, but certain practices in the business world apply here. Although requesting a resume or letters of recommendation from a community volunteer is unnecessary in this context, the principles behind them work. Keep in mind that the mere kindness of someone's offering to speak to students is not enough to ensure professional quality. Above all, particularly in the case of persons with little or no prior experience speaking to children, it is essential to determine that the speaker has something special to offer elementary students. Get recommendations from colleagues who have already heard the speaker or inquire about his or her prior engagements. To follow up on that response, it is entirely appropriate to call the previous host. By courteously inquiring about the general success of the program and asking about the strengths of the guest speaker, the conversation remains positive and invites the host to state comfortably and honestly whether the speaker met expectations. In many cases, it is helpful to meet with the potential speaker prior to establishing a definite commitment for the program. To review, following are general questions to consider when selecting a guest speaker:

- Is the speaker knowledgeable about the topic?

- Will the speaker be interesting to children?

- Has the speaker worked with children before?

- Does the speaker seem to grasp the focus and purpose of the program?

- Have others recommended this speaker as valuable?

- Does the speaker seem willing to work within the program demands?

As a general rule, the most important question to consider is: If I were a student required to sit through this speaker's presentation, would I learn and have fun at the same time?

Sue Wiley invited a former rodeo competitor to speak to the fourth-graders.

A "real cowboy" came highly recommended by a teacher from my school who had previously heard him speak to young people. I began our conversation by simply sharing some of my program plans. His responses assured me of not only his subject knowledge, but also his expertise on the specific program content. As it turned out, he knew a lot about nearly everything I was hoping a speaker would share. But what really sold me on him was how his enthusiasm animated him as he spoke. With interesting information and a personality that I thought fourth-graders would surely love, I had found my guest speaker.

To find speakers, start searching near the school. The local community is filled with possible resources. Professionals at nearby businesses are often glad to share their time and expertise. For both their work experience and hobbies, parents are also a wellspring of opportunity. Refer to Chapter 4 for more detailed and extensive information about locating a guest speaker. Also, numerous Web sites for various resources that may provide connections to speakers are listed in Chapter 6.

One major consideration when selecting a guest speaker for an event is availability. When first meeting the resource person or talking on the telephone with him or her, get some sense of when that person will be available to participate in the program. If a particular date and location are already planned, share that information. If this date conflicts with the speaker's schedule, suggest one of the alternate dates still open on the school events calendar. After selecting a speaker, describe to him or her the following program details:

- Date and time
- Location of presentation
- Program goals
- Program content
- Length of time for the program
- Age of the audience
- Size of the audience
- Equipment and software needs (including microphone)
- Accessory needs (such as podium, screen, dry board, and markers)

One week prior to the event, help your resource person by doing the following:

- Provide a final written reminder of the date, time, and location.
- Reiterate the importance of being on time.
- Remind him or her of the amount of time allotted.
- Confirm that you have obtained needed equipment and requested resources.

Finally, follow up with a friendly telephone call several days before the event to ensure the speaker knows his or her obligations and is ready to fulfill them.

Because a guest speaker is an integral part of the program, obtaining a firm commitment is the first step in solidifying the tentative plans made earlier. Immediately after a guest speaker confirms his or her participation, lock in the program time on the school calendar. Because so many special events occur throughout a school year, other faculty members may be vying for some of those same times. Confirming that date immediately after it is decided with the guest speaker not only assures that the program will happen then but also frees up the alternative dates for colleagues waiting to plan a special event (like a sports tournament, fair, or field trip).

Select and Provide for Support Personnel

After selecting the main guest speaker, find and secure any other participants needed to carry out the program. Other guest participants, parent volunteers, and faculty members are among the people you might need to help shoulder the responsibilities of executing the program. The number of students attending and number of activities planned are the two main criteria for determining how many participants and helpers are appropriate. Finding assistants is similar to, yet not quite as demanding as, selecting the primary guest speaker. Regardless of their role, be sure to meet with all participants and make certain they are knowledgeable concerning the topic. Also ensure that each individual can relate to the students. Although not as critical as the main guest speaker who will be commanding the students' attention, the other participants help set the tone for the event. Volunteers and assistants who help students feel comfortable and successful will greatly enhance the impression students leave with by the program's end.

Select, Order, and Schedule Resource Materials

Materials to support the program include the children's books, reference materials, professional materials for teachers, media, computer and audiovisual equipment, Internet Web sites, and any other materials related to the topic. (Chapter 4 focuses on how to identify resources.) Begin searching for support materials on the topic in your own school library media center, other media centers in the district, and in the district professional library (if one is available). Then go out into the community, where resource persons, businesses, and organizations can provide support materials. Sometimes a program may require purchasing some books and materials related to the topic.

Identifying resources and their availability early (see Chapter 2) determines the feasibility of your program idea. Being familiar with existing resources on the topic allows you to select, order, and schedule materials. When selecting resources, consider the following factors:

- Is the content of the resource related to the program theme?
- Is the resource appropriate for the age level of the target group?
- Is the resource of interest to the target group?
- Is the resource current?
- Is the resource easily accessible?
- What is the cost of the resource (if any)?

Some media specialists begin planning an event a year in advance, particularly when they are planning an extravaganza such as the 25th anniversary of the school. This advance planning allows media specialists to make the most of their ordering of books and media in the spring or scheduling the rental of free-standing exhibits and multimedia programs. When there is not time to put in an order to publishers or jobbers, media specialists find it necessary to purchase materials at their local bookstore or through the Internet.

Sue Wiley was excited about the prospect of ordering a traveling exhibit on Texas cowboys from a state museum.

I knew the exhibit would be a terrific addition to my program. Unfortunately, when submitting my request, I learned that exhibits from institutions and organizations are sometimes scheduled a year in advance. The one I wanted was unavailable. Though disappointed, I chose a worthwhile alternative: I developed an original exhibit that included a saddle and blanket, branding iron, and lariat loaned by the generous fifth-grade teacher and my guest speaker.

I also added new program elements to the event. A favorite was getting a parent volunteer to demonstrate how to make beef jerky. Our brainstorming session resulted in a clever program addition. She could serve the beef jerky from a miniature chuck wagon placed in the library media center. Students would visit the chuck wagon, watch the demonstration, and then receive a piece of beef jerky and the recipe for making it at home.

As my program grew, all program elements except the rodeo video began flowing into a smooth, logical progression. Yet the video was so good I hated to omit it. Instead, I offered fourth-grade teachers the option of bringing their students to the media center for a special viewing of the video a few days before my program. To give the video presentation more meaning, I offered classroom teachers a written rationale for showing the film. I also provided them with a list of questions for students to answer after viewing the film and returning to their classrooms.

Develop Contingency Plans

Be prepared for problems. When planning large programs it is inevitable that something unanticipated will occur. Even with small programs, have an alternate plan in mind if the speaker cancels. After confirming a date for smaller programs, determine a backup date that is also acceptable in case an unforeseen conflict arises. For larger events that require staying with the single date on the school events calendar, the alternate plan must involve preparing backup activities ready. In either case, communicate clearly to all participants that it is imperative for them to notify you immediately if any problem occurs. Setting clear expectations can prevent some problems, but inevitable frustrations like unexpected illness or uncooperative weather make it always essential to have a contingency plan ready to execute.

Despite being new to planning major programs, Sue Wiley had the foresight to prepare for some potential problems.

> One thing I did right on my first program was to plan alternate exhibits and activities in case one failed. I also selected a second video (not as good as the first) to serve as a back-up for the scheduled media presentation. One thing I would do differently would be to plan an alternate activity in case my "real cowboy" didn't show. Because I didn't have a backup plan to replace him, I kept my fingers crossed that he would make the important date. Thinking back on it, I would have rested easier if I had an alternate program, like another presentation, available for the program date just in case the speaker canceled.

COMPLETING
FINAL PREPARATIONS

Once the preliminary plans have been completed for the content; resources; and an exact location, time, and date for the event, it is time to plan for the day of the program.

Identify, Select, and Prepare Student and Parent Volunteers

Media specialists are usually desperate for volunteers who can help on the day of the program, but they also need them before and after the event. Usually parents and community members who are regular volunteers in the school library media center are enlisted. For special programs, some media specialists choose to reach out to parents other than the regular volunteers by phoning parents who earlier indicated an interest in volunteering at special events. They may also ask the PTA or PTO to support the program by finding volunteers for this one occasion. Regardless of how volunteers are recruited, they will help ensure that the event runs smoothly. (see Photo 3.1)

Photo 3.1. Media specialist Julie Godfrey prepares the volunteers for the upcoming program related to her book fair extravaganza. (*Memorial Drive Elementary School, Houston, Texas, Spring Branch Independent School District*)

After securing volunteers, conduct a short meeting with the group or speak to them individually to help them feel clear about, and comfortable with, their responsibilities during the program. At the meeting be sure to

- provide an overview of the upcoming program, including date and time,

- find out what each volunteer is interested in doing,

- discuss the tasks required of each volunteer,

- make certain all volunteers understand that they will work during the preparation stages as well as on the day of the program,

- give volunteers an opportunity to choose what they want to do,

- get to know the volunteers to make certain they are matched with appropriate tasks, and

- work to excite the volunteers about the program.

Tasks that can be handled by volunteers before the day of the event include

- helping with publicity (make posters, signs, and banners; write articles for the newspaper),
- researching the topic,
- helping locate resources,
- assisting in developing book displays,
- decorating the facility,
- helping create enrichment activities to follow the program, and
- helping to design learning centers.

Tasks for volunteers to do on the day of the program or during the program include

- arranging furniture for the program,
- operating audiovisual equipment and computers,
- serving as hosts and greeting guests,
- monitoring traffic flow,
- helping with lighting, and
- reminding classes of assigned times to arrive at the program.

Sue knew from the moment she decided to plan an extravaganza that volunteers would be the key to making her program a success.

By including so many different program designs, including displays, exhibits, centers, and the featured speaker, I knew I either needed to find some volunteer helpers or sacrifice some of the activities. Even knowing that I could use my five permanent volunteers, I still needed more support. So I pulled out my volunteer file and read through the questionnaires that had been returned by parents at the beginning of the school year. Then I asked one of my permanent volunteers to call the parents who had expressed interest in volunteering for special events. After we found three who were willing to help, I decided to continue with my entire program plan.

Publicize the Event

Successful programs require advertising. Because students are the intended audience, work toward exciting them about the event. Early on, get the backing of the principal and teachers. Their enthusiasm will help inspire students.

Begin publicizing at least three weeks before the event. Besides building excitement, publicity improves the image of the school library media center in the eyes of the teachers, students, parents, and community. An underlying objective of any program is to get children interested in the school library media center, and inspire them to return. Thus, let your publicity highlight the exciting opportunities awaiting students in the media center. Effective programs often motivate students to return later in the week to check out books or use reference materials on the subject. Of all long-term benefits, motivating students to use the media center regularly is the greatest.

Programs in the school library media center give media specialists an opportunity to show off their facility to the community as well. When planning an event, invite the local newspaper or television station. Let everyone in the community, particularly parents, know and understand what their school library media center offers. Beyond general advertisements, send letters to parents announcing the event created for their children.

Publicity within the school can include posters, daily announcements, newsletters, and, if the school has one, marquee advertisements. Let students contribute to the public relations campaign by designing their own posters. Many media specialists even sponsor poster contests. Allow students to design personalized invitations for parents, administrators, and community members. Newsletters can also work wonders.

Consider advertising the event in the school newspaper. If publications also exist at the district level, promote your school, and yourself, by notifying the district communications department about the upcoming event. If possible, let students help write your press releases. Besides helping you, it offers them a unique learning experience.

Prepare Students and Teachers for the Event

In some cases, you alone can target your publicity to teachers and students. For other programs, secure teacher help. Ask them to provide the students with background information on the topic prior to the speaker, demonstration, or exhibit. For example, a media specialist in Nashville invited a guest author to her school. Before the major event, she gave fourth-grade teachers paperback books by that writer. Students were also asked to find biographical information about the author. This preparation built anticipation for meeting the author in both the students as well as the teachers.

Sometimes media specialists prepare the teachers and students by sharing information about an author's life and works during the regularly scheduled library classes. In the school that Jack Prelutsky visited, the principal read one of his poems over the intercom each day of the week before the event. Selected by the media specialist, the hilarious poems generated program interest more effectively than other, costlier promotional ideas. Also, this entertaining promotion subtly provided the background information students needed to enjoy the program. Further information taught by the media specialist and the teachers made students more than adequately prepared for the event.

Schedule Classes

Scheduling classes for a program can be challenging. Programs targeted at only one grade level are relatively simple to schedule, but more ambitious programs require more planning and coordinating. Whatever the target audience is, involve teachers in the scheduling process from the beginning. Teachers tend to be more flexible if they have been involved in program planning and are in support of the program event from the start. The positive rapport you perpetuate with teachers will surely help when requesting their flexibility and cooperation. Scheduling possibilities for programs vary according to program type.

- If the program features displays or exhibits, classes can come through at their convenience or sign up to visit the display or exhibit.

- If the program focuses on learning or interest centers, the classes can be scheduled to participate in the center. Or, students may come from their classrooms with a pass, or in some cases visit the centers at their own convenience.

- If the program includes a guest speaker who will demonstrate or speak to one class or grade level, the students must attend the program at the designated time. (During the early planning process, the media specialist will have selected a time that was agreeable to the grade-level team or classroom teacher.)

- If the program is intended for the entire student body, seek scheduling help. At larger schools, such events are generally offered as part of a greater schoolwide event, such as an assembly or fair. At a smaller school, you may choose to host a grand event on your own. In either case, ambitious programs require collaboration by faculty, administration, and even staff.

Whatever schedule is used, remind teachers about it, up to the very morning of the event:

- Send out reminders on attractive flyers.

- Post reminders in the teachers' lounge.

- Enlist volunteers to help remind teachers about the schedule.

- Make an announcement over the intercom the day before, and the day of, the event.

ARRANGING THE FACILITY

An attractive facility adds vitality to the program and sets the tone. To enhance the atmosphere of your school library media center, decorate, rearrange furniture, and modify the general appearance of the facility to fit your program needs. (see Photo 3.2)

Photo 3.2. Exhibits of student art on bulletin boards welcome students to the school library media center. *(Edward White Elementary School, El Lago, Texas, Clear Creek Independent School District)*

Decorate

Bulletin boards build excitement for upcoming events, then serve as learning tools during the program. Displaying books or objects related to the event also enhance the learning environment. Decorations, such as balloons and student art, add to the festivity of the event.

Collaborate with classroom teachers to enhance your program setting. Students enjoy creating posters and banners to make the facility more attractive. They are especially proud to see their art or essays on display. Piñatas, mobiles, and student art that hang from the ceiling make dramatic, eye-catching impressions.

Sue Wiley tied "Rodeos and Cowboys" to the Houston Livestock Show and Rodeo Art Contest by sponsoring a similar contest in her own library.

While proceeding with my program plans, I read about the Rodeo Art contest. Working with that idea, I found a way to open my program to the entire school by inviting all students to enter the contest. The third-grade teachers who were disappointed previously now seemed happier that their students could contribute, even if they would not attend.

I sent a flyer home with each student describing the contest. I kept the rules simple to encourage creativity. The response was encouraging. I received wonderful artwork to tack on the walls and papier-mâché horses to hang from the ceiling. With my book displays and exhibits, the facility became a varied and exciting program setting.

Use Technology Support

Occasionally, programs are presented entirely through technology. For example, the rodeo video that Sue Wiley showed fourth-graders was itself a form of programming. Most often, technology supports a program by providing the equipment and software necessary for the presenter to share information.

Media specialists must make arrangements for the equipment and software ahead of time. Often, providing a reminder to the presenters concerning copyright laws helps ensure that strict adherence to the laws is honored. Some equipment must be scheduled weeks in advance. When using multimedia, consider the following questions:

- What equipment do the participants need?
- Will the participants provide their own equipment?

- Is the requested equipment in good working order?
- Where will the equipment be placed?
- Are backup equipment and extra bulbs available and handy?
- Do the participants want a podium or table and chair?
- Will the equipment need to be moved during the program?
- What software is required?
- Do the participants need a chalkboard, easel, or chart?
- Are extension cords needed?
- Do the participants need someone to operate the equipment for them?
- Who will take care of lighting?

Well before the day of the program, determine the type of equipment that the guests will need and whether they will need help operating it. If they choose to operate the equipment themselves, on the day of the program make certain they feel comfortable with the equipment before the program begins.

The day before the event, set up any required audiovisual equipment, computers, microphones, screens, and software. Ensure that everything works, that sound levels of all audio equipment can be heard throughout the facility, and if used, that screens are visible from every seat.

Arrange Furniture and Seating

Ideally, the furniture should be arranged the day before the program. If this is impossible, at least have a drawing of the room arrangement so volunteers can help arrange the furniture on the day of the event. Questions to answer concerning the furniture and seating arrangement include:

- How many students and guests will attend?
- Will the children sit on chairs or on the floor?
- Does the speaker have any special needs regarding seating arrangements or speaker podium?
- Where will the speaker stand?
- Will the speaker need a microphone?
- Will the speaker need a projection screen?
- Where will the media specialist sit?

- Will grade levels sit together?

- Should the younger children be seated in front of the older?

- Where will the teachers sit?

- Where will the guests sit?

- Does seating need to be provided for the participants?

- Where should the furniture be placed?

- Who will help arrange the furniture?

- Who will help put the furniture back following the program?

Provide for Traffic Flow

Programs that involve only a few classes will not create major traffic flow problems. However, for larger programs that involve the entire school, the media specialist must make arrangements for traffic flow several days before the program. The following questions should be considered:

- At what time do the students begin arriving?

- At what time should all students be seated?

- How much time is needed to get all students to the area designated for the program?

- In what order will the classes arrive?

- Do some classes have special needs or considerations that must be addressed in advance? (For example, will students with physical disabilities need to leave early?)

- Are a sufficient number of volunteers or student aides available to help supervise the traffic flow?

To address some of these concerns, Sue Wiley met with her program volunteers to discuss traffic flow. Even that late in the planning, new ideas improved her program.

One parent suggested that all volunteers come to the event dressed in western clothes. Besides enhancing the overall atmosphere, their attire made them easily identifiable to students who followed their directions for finding a seat, moving past the exhibits, and returning to their classrooms.

EXECUTING THE PROGRAM

For events requiring one or more speakers, the following tasks should be completed on the day before or the day of the event:

- Remind teachers and students of program time and their seating time.
- Remind volunteers about the times and scheduling.
- Complete final seating arrangements.
- Check the environment: temperature, lighting, and ventilation.
- Review with the volunteers their assigned tasks.
- Make certain the speakers' requests have been met before their arrival.
- Greet the speakers.
- Make sure the speakers are comfortable with the equipment, room arrangement, and program agenda and schedule.
- Review with the speakers the importance of staying on the time schedule (and perhaps a signal to end the presentation).
- Spend some time after the program with the guests (coffee, lunch, a short visit).

Present the Program

Regardless of the program size or complexity, perform each of the following steps:

- Begin at the scheduled time.
- Introduce the event by giving background information on the special event.
- Recognize all the people who made it possible.
- Remind students of expectations for behavior (for example, when during the program it is appropriate for them to ask questions).
- Introduce the guest speaker.
- Monitor the students during the presentation.
- Motion to the speaker if he or she goes over time.
- When the speaker has finished, thank him or her for the presentation and thank everyone for attending.

- Provide the students and teachers with directions on how they should leave the facility.

Follow Through After the Event

Even after the event, the program is not complete without appropriate reinforcement. To ensure that the students get the most out of the program, the media specialist and the teachers should provide students with follow-up activities. These activities must review or extend the information shared during the program. Below are tips for providing student enrichment:

- Consider a follow-up event on the same topic.

- Make books on related topics available for checkout.

- Make media on related topics available to teachers.

- Provide enrichment activities in the school library media center (learning centers, displays).

- Provide related library skills lessons during the students' library classes.

- Encourage and give suggestions for individual classroom activities.

- Provide both students and teachers with bibliographies of related student resources.

- Provide teachers with a bibliography of related professional materials.

- Request feedback from the students and teachers about the program (see Chapter 7 for details).

CONCLUSION

If the thought of developing a program for the school library media center seems as overwhelming as it is exciting, think about starting with a program that involves only one speaker for a particular grade level. For something simpler, create a learning center or interest center around an intriguing theme. Consider renting (for a nominal fee) a predesigned display from a museum or cultural organization for your first program. Create an interactive bulletin board or display. From there, let the programs grow. With inspiration from small successes first, any library media specialist can coordinate multifaceted programs that promote the media center and the school and make a dynamic, lasting impression on any group of students. (see Figure 3.1, page 64, for a complete checklist for a successful program)

PROGRAM CHECKLIST

Several Months Prior to Event
_____ Decide on theme/topic
_____ Develop objectives
_____ Identify available resources

One Month Prior to Event
_____ Obtain permission from administration
_____ Select participants
_____ Select materials
_____ Identify audience, date, and time
_____ Contact participants
_____ Begin publicizing event
_____ Develop contingency plans:
_____ Alternate dates
_____ Alternate activities
_____ Alternate speakers

One to Two Weeks Prior to Event
_____ Schedule volunteers
_____ Determine seating arrangements
_____ Determine traffic flow
_____ Give teachers schedule of event
_____ At faculty meeting, discuss event (problems, schedules, etc.)
_____ Determine participants' technology needs

One Day Prior to Event
_____ Prepare seating arrangement
_____ Prepare audiovisual equipment
_____ Prepare decorations, displays, and exhibits
_____ Remind volunteers and participants of time
_____ Remind teachers of schedule

Day of Event
Conduct a last-minute check of facility:
_____ Room temperature
_____ Lighting
_____ Room arrangement
_____ Audiovisual equipment and cords
_____ Speaker podium
_____ Seating arrangement
_____ Inform volunteers of duties
_____ Greet speakers

After Event
_____ Conduct an informal evaluation
_____ Conduct a formal evaluation
_____ Send letters of appreciation to participants
_____ Analyze program

Figure 3.1. Checklist for successful programs.

Chapter 4

How to Identify and Locate Resources

Once she determined her program theme, Sue Wiley began gathering resources.

Step one in executing my program goals was getting resources. I set out to find: an authentic rodeo participant for my guest speaker, a cook to demonstrate how to make beef jerky, a display of western items, the video about the rodeo, and plenty of student-made art work.

Requesting these items at a faculty meeting proved fruitful. One teacher connected me with a former rodeo competitor. A fifth-grade teacher, who lived on a ranch, offered to share a branding iron, saddle, saddle blanket, halter, lariat, chaps, and a hat. From that one simple announcement to my colleagues, I found my primary resource (the speaker), and enough materials to decorate my media center or create an exhibit. It was a valuable lesson. I did not need to venture out alone to put together a fine program. Simply requesting help from coworkers can harvest great results.

Resource people and materials abound. With a little knowledge and ingenuity, it's easy to locate materials to support your program.

IDENTIFYING AND
LOCATING RESOURCES

From the onset, your search will teach you what types of resources exist, who has them, and when they're available. At first, your options may be overwhelmingly broad. But during the process, you'll quickly learn to specify your needs, make useful contacts, and determine which resource options are best for your program. Begin by answering these three questions:

1. What do I want?

2. What can I afford?

3. When do I need it?

The answers to these questions jump-start a fruitful and productive search.

Educational Resources

Begin gathering resources from your library media center. Often books and materials in your own collection inspire your program ideas or clarify your program focus. Because you know your collection, gathering books and materials should be simple. Seeing what you have on hand determines how deep and extensive your subsequent search must be.

From there, expand your search incrementally. A little investigating may reveal that colleagues on your campus have expertise or collections perfect for your program. A teacher or administrator may be your best choice for guest speaker. Why go through the process of finding, interviewing, and inviting an unfamiliar speaker from the community when many of your colleagues, who relate to children for a living and will be on campus anyway, could enthusiastically share their knowledge about a favorite topic?

As you continue your search, consider district administrators, subject area coordinators, and, most importantly, other library media specialists. Next, explore possibilities in the community. Not surprisingly, the challenge at that stage is not locating the resources, but selecting the best for your program needs.

Children's Books

Books are integral to all school library media programs. Often, a book or books will be the program topic. Even if your event focuses on developing a skill, such as learning some new technology, include books. Have them handy for introducing information before and during the program, and make them available after the program to extend learning.

Because encouraging lifelong readers is a primary goal of education, books should be a central component to any program.

Many media specialists rely on more than only the books in their collection. Before the program, some specialists borrow books through interlibrary loan to gather their information, and to have the books available for check out after the program. Once you begin developing long-term visions for future programs, you can budget for and order resources to have on hand when you are ready to plan the event.

Professional Materials

When gathering resources for programs, search your campus or district professional collection. Many of these books and journals explore education theory and share creative classroom activities. From them, you may find worthwhile information to supplement programs for students, or professional growth activities to use for programs directed to faculty.

A few district-level professional libraries offer research services. They can locate professional articles on your program topic, identify information about authors, direct Internet searches, or secure appointments from available speakers. If they cannot make arrangements for you, they may have a community resources file that includes possible speakers for programs. Finally, district libraries also lend other support materials, including films and computer software.

Remember, colleagues may have resources in their departments that you would not normally keep in your media center. Physical education equipment, history games, lab equipment, and class sets of novels could supplement a program in their respective subject areas.

Audiovisual Materials

Like any lesson, a program should meet the needs of visual, auditory, and kinesthetic learners. Eye-catching visuals, appealing graphics, and appropriate audio elements hold students' attention and enhance learning. After you have decided what audiovisuals to incorporate into your program, begin gathering resources from your own collection. Videos, books on tape, and CD-ROMs that you initially ordered for classroom use may meet your program needs. As suggested previously, expand your search incrementally. Ask department or team leaders if they have resources you need. If you have a regional distribution center that loans AV, check their catalog or Web site and order what you want well before the program. You need time to preview the work to determine its quality and decide what parts you will include in the program. Also, you don't want to risk not having the material on your program date. Better to get it early and request an extension than to discover that your well-timed order was never filled.

Consider also AV material you wish to create. Attractive overheads are the perfect complement to many school library media programs. Because they combine information, visual movement, and sound effects, PowerPoint presentations are outstanding teaching tools. Sometimes filming your own video personalizes the learning for students, especially if some have contributed to the effort. For example, when a media specialist in Oklahoma could not find a video that succinctly explained tools of early Native Americans, she and some students videotaped a demonstration with props and artifacts she had collected.

Once you determine your AV needs, set aside or reserve equipment. You probably have much of what you need already. Gather it together and check it out to yourself. You don't want an assistant or volunteer to unknowingly issue the equipment to a teacher just as you are prepared to use it. If a teacher already has equipment you want for your program, arrange early to get it back, or negotiate a plan to have a volunteer retrieve and return it.

More expensive equipment, such as an LCD projector, may be more difficult to acquire. Some districts purchase one such item and then make it available to all campuses, or limit its use to the administrative offices only. Get an up-to-date list of your district's AV, and the ordering policy. Waiting lists can make it impossible to secure the equipment you want unless you've requested it several months earlier.

Check with other school library media specialists. Some colleagues work closely together, each agreeing to order different AV equipment and then share it among campuses. Others have a central budget controlled by an administrative coordinator. At the very least, suggest that all media specialists in your district list the AV equipment they have and are willing to share, then distribute those lists at the next meeting. Having immediate access to this list can save time as you gather program resources.

Teacher- and Student-made Resources

As an educator, you probably create some support material from scratch. Making your own program resources, alone or with teachers and students, can benefit everyone and be economical for you. It can offer teachers a new focus to a familiar lesson. It can provide students a creative activity and a chance to contribute to a major event. For example, instead of requiring students to color a map in social studies, a teacher in Connecticut asked them to help her arrange materials in a jackdaw (see Appendix C). They gave their completed project to the media specialist, who used it during a program, then displayed it in the media center afterward. The resources you seek may be easily acquired. If not, they may be worth making.

Story Aprons

While reading to students, teachers can use flannel boards to display and manipulate objects related to the story. Although these stationary boards are appropriate for small groups, media specialists often need more mobility when presenting programs. Story aprons serve the same purpose as flannel boards, but use an apron as the display surface. Affix objects representing characters or details from the story to the apron with Velcro, magnets, or adhesive. While reading or telling a story, you may use the objects to clarify details and introduce a multi-sensory dimension to your program. These teacher-made or commercial aprons are versatile, durable, and popular with students. See Photo 4.1 and Appendix C for complete instructions for developing story aprons.

Photo 4.1 University student prepares to share a story using her creative story apron with elementary youngsters in a local school library media center. (*University of Houston-Clear Lake, Houston, Texas*)

Puppets

When considering program resources, do not overlook a common prop for elementary school events: puppets. Whether designed commercially, by teachers, or by students, puppets are versatile teaching tools. Some school library media centers even house permanent stages designed specifically for puppet shows. Occasionally, puppet stages are set on wheels so that teachers can check them out and move them to their own classrooms.

Jackdaws

Some library media specialists may be unfamiliar with jackdaws. These teacher-made or commercially produced learning tools often support social studies activities. A jackdaw is any type of portfolio used as a learning tool. They usually contain reproductions of historical documents, maps, photos, and other interesting educational materials that bring to life a period of history. Jackdaws are frequently paired with children's historical fiction, biographies, or information books. They also can be used to support programs on various topics. For example, before reading a biography about Abraham Lincoln, a media specialist shared a jackdaw containing photographs of Lincoln, a Civil War map, miniature Union and Confederate flags, and a weathered copy of the Emancipation Proclamation.

Besides being attractive and useful, jackdaws are easy to store. Although some media specialists keep jackdaws only for their programs and displays, others catalog them and allow teachers to check them out for classroom use. When planning a program for teachers, note that "Creating Jackdaws" is an excellent topic. Jackdaws are simple to compile, versatile, and, still unfamiliar to many teachers. Appendix C gives examples and a complete description of how to develop jackdaws.

Student Art

Include student art in the school library media center. It is decorative, and students are proud to see their work displayed. Art supplements larger programs, or may be the focus of a bulletin board or exhibit. You may also want to change student art displays as an ongoing program. Using this idea, one media specialist listed seven themes appropriate for different months. When school began, she asked each grade level (K-6) team to choose one month and have students create art related to its corresponding theme. Each month, teachers submitted their students' work to the media center, where parent volunteers showcased the art on a large, decorated wall.

Art Program Titles

October	Favorite Jack-o'-Lantern Designs (second grade)
November	Don't be a Turkey (fifth grade)
December	Holiday Wishes (sixth grade)
January	Jack Frost's Snowflakes (fourth grade)
February	Old-fashioned Valentines (third grade)
March	Raining Cats and Dogs (first grade)
April	Velveteen Rabbits (kindergarten)

Dioramas

Dioramas can also help school library media centers come to life. Encourage students to make dioramas in lieu of book reports. After reading individual books, students can take an empty shoe box and depict a memorable scene using pictures from magazines, three-dimensional objects, and drawings. Have students cover the opening with clear wrap, and label their project with their name, book title and author. Place the dioramas on tables and shelves throughout your media center. Students enjoy seeing their own creations and the work of their classmates. Ideally, some dioramas may motivate students to check out and read the books depicted.

Community Resources

Regardless of its size, every community can offer schools many human and material resources. Finding them depends upon what people, places, holidays and special events exist in a community. Remember, community resources can dominate or supplement programming.

For her program entitled "Behind the Scenes with a Magician," a media specialist invited an amateur magician to teach students magic tricks. Other programs may require only supplemental support from the community. One media specialist presented a program called "Care for Your Pet." Afterward, she distributed pamphlets donated by a local veterinarian.

For this part of your search especially, be systematic. Chart a course for identifying and locating resources. Decide what you want, then list logical providers. Knowing budget, time, and space parameters will also help you decide what resources to pursue.

(Figure 4.1 depicts a summary of the ways media specialists and other educators can identify the types of resources that enrich and support programs.)

Ways to Locate Resources	
Type of Resource	**Sources**
Resource People	Questionnaire (see Figure 5.1) PTA or PTO Faculty recommendations Public library
Interesting Places	*Chamber of Commerce* City guides Internet (see Chapter 6)
Institutions	*Telephone directory* Internet (see Chapter 6) Teacher/parent recommendations
Business and Industry	*Telephone directory* Chamber of Commerce Internet (see Chapter 6) Teacher/parent recommendations
Organizations and Clubs	*Chamber of Commerce* Directories Internet (see Chapter 6) Teacher/parent recommendation
Government Agencies	*Internet* (see Chapter 6) Telephone directory
Special Events and Holidays	*Chamber of Commerce* News media
Children's Literature	*Selection aids* Media specialists, teachers, children Professional journal articles
Professional Materials	*Children's literature resources* (see Appendix E)
Displays and Exhibits	*Phoning community resources* Media resources (magazines, television) Internet (see Chapter 6) Other libraries

Figure 4.1. Ways to locate resources.

Below are resources available in most communities. Beyond these suggestions, consider resources unique to your community because of local traditions and businesses.

Resource People

In every school and community, many resource persons are eager to share knowledge, skills, and special interests with young people. While searching, begin with the easiest to find: parents, teachers, and students in your own school. Many parents and faculty members are eager to share special talents, leisure activities, travel experiences, and career information. Whether the media specialist needs a guest speaker or an interesting collection to feature in a display case, these resource persons can provide excellent enrichment at usually no cost.

Consider professionals in the community (including parents) as possible speakers. Medical doctors, nurses, veterinarians, architects, attorneys, pilots, flight attendants, scientists, engineers, and many others who frequently participate in career days may be receptive to speaking at other special programs.

Employees of institutions, businesses, and government agencies are usually top-level contacts. Retirees are just as valuable and may be easier to schedule. Consider specialized groups, from sewing circles to bird watchers to athletic organizations. Enthusiastic volunteers from any profession or interest group can offer children enrichment on a variety of subjects.

Interesting Places

Some media specialists are so familiar with their community, they overlook special places that can enrich programming. Major tourist attractions, historical buildings, government offices, landmarks, parks, gardens, fountains, and even shopping malls have a history and character that define a community. Although such sites inspire great field trips, they can also enrich school library media programs by providing speakers, display materials, exhibits, and information.

Institutions

Institutions throughout the community can support programs related to elementary curriculum and student interests. (Figure 4.2, page 74, lists some institutions common to most communities along with related program titles.)

Institutions	Program Titles
University	Reviewing Children's Books (professor presents program to faculty)
Zoo	Cold-blooded Animals (docent brings animals and discusses each)
Museum	What the Children's Museum Has to Offer Teachers (volunteer from museum shares information)
Hospital	Avoiding the Common Cold (nurse presents information)
Bank	How Money Is Made (bank employee shares information)
Library	Getting a Public Library Card (librarian presents to fifth and sixth graders)

Figure 4.2. Examples of institutions with program titles.

Universities and colleges provide especially good resources. While reading about or attending university events, consider how they might enrich an elementary school program. Also watch for interesting programs sponsored by universities. Author presentations, musical performances, and art exhibits can inspire program ideas. Realize also that university recruiters who work with high schools can easily adapt career guidance programs to the elementary level.

Zoos, museums, and planetariums make ideal field trip experiences, and they support schools in other ways. Some provide great presenters through their speaker bureau. Many lend freestanding exhibits or traveling trunks that may contain manipulatives, artifacts, costumes, information packets, teaching suggestions, and student activities. Often, these educational tools are provided free. Some institutions even hire out entire self-contained programs. For example, zoo mobiles travel to schools where animal experts share information while allowing students to pet various mammals, snakes, and birds.

Health-related topics, ranging from disease prevention and hygiene to functions of the human body, make informative school library media programs. Hospitals can provide guest speakers, print material, and exhibits that enhance programming. Likewise, area banks can offer schools interesting speakers and print resources. For example, a bank in

Florida sends out employees to speak at school functions on topics ranging from "How Money Is Made" to "Counterfeiting: a Costly Crime."
Commonly, doctors, nurses, dentists, bankers, and other resources connected to institutions are often willing to discuss their professions with
students on career days.

Naturally, public and county libraries, as well as school library
media centers in school districts, can give media specialists a wealth of
information and resources for programming. Minimize your work load
by securing community resources. Often, program ideas and materials
have already been gathered by an institution that specializes in your program topic.

Other Libraries

While searching for resources to support your program, examine
other community resource files. These include:

- Other elementary school library media centers within the
  district

- Middle or high school library media centers within the district

- Professional materials collection at the Teacher Center (if
  available)

- Public library

Occasionally, you will discover a diverse, full, and current community resource file maintained by a colleague. When accessing such a
treasure, discuss programming ideas and resources with the other media
specialist. Public libraries routinely offer programs for children, so check
out the library's newsletter and note titles of various program offerings.
By joining the public library's Friends organization, one media specialist
learned about many types of programs offered to young patrons. She
was able to use some of the same community resources and adapt many
ideas for her own school library media programming.

Business and Industry

To fulfill community service responsibilities, many businesses collaborate with area schools, some even forming partnerships with specific
campuses. This service includes contributing to school library media
programs. Businesses can support special programs by providing guest
speakers, media software, print resources, or even financial support for
events. Often, large companies have entire PR departments willing to
work with media specialists.

Companies sometimes give schools pre-constructed exhibits,
ready for display. If using displays or exhibit materials from businesses,

always present a balanced approach to the topic and never promote a single company, no matter how generous their contribution to your program.

Taking three precautions can prevent problems.

1. Avoid advertising a particular product or company. Because it would be unreasonable to satisfy all competitors in a specific field, keep exhibits generic rather than brand-name specific. If this is impossible, randomly display a variety of brands without favoring any one.

2. Sidestep controversial topics unless prepared to include every point of view. Although it is important to offer a balanced view of any topic, controversial ones can leave you especially vulnerable, especially if the topic touches a nerve for any group in your community. If you like to tackle controversial issues, allow all opposing sides equal time to share views.

3. Protect any materials used in programming. Most damaged or lost books can easily be replaced; program materials are often unique, rare, and to some who share them, irreplaceable. Take no chances. Secure materials in a locked display case when appropriate, or develop safety precautions that work at your facility. Whenever ordering or gathering materials, anticipate potential problems and respond to each accordingly.

Whether securing the support of one company representative or an entire PR department, realize that working with companies is mutually beneficial. By contributing to your program, they generate good PR and enhance their reputation in the community. (Figure 4.3 lists businesses that frequently support programs in the elementary school and related program titles.)

Businesses	Program Titles
Travel agency	Oriental Journey
Veterinarian's office	Caring for Your Pet
Bookstore	Pop-up Books
Restaurant	What Does a Chef Do?
Bakery	How Donuts Are Made
Car dealer	How Automobiles Are Made

Figure 4.3. Examples of businesses and related program titles.

Besides contacting the companies and businesses listed in Figure 4.3, consider the following:

computer store	electric companies
interior design firm	doctor's office
pet store	law firm
ethnic food store	telephone company
grocery store	home repair business
boat and yacht business	plumbing business
sporting goods store	landscaping business
gas company	home building company
drug store	architectural firm
marketing company	department store
railroad company	beauty salon
automobile dealer	dental office
airlines	hardware store

Clubs and Organizations

Community clubs and organizations cover an array of interests. Because these organizations and clubs often focus on specific areas of interest, their members may be uniquely qualified to share expertise on topics related to your program.

Special interest clubs and organizations can be far-reaching. Sports clubs provide a perfect example of how far-reaching your resources can be. To gain program support related to athletics, you may begin by contacting a major sports organization. If having no personal connections to a sports franchise becomes an obstacle, realize that some of your colleagues may be perfect liaisons between you and a professional organization.

For example, one media specialist had trouble finding a professional baseball player to speak at an event. After expressing frustration with a colleague, she learned that one of the district's baseball coaches was a former major league outfielder. Not only did the coach offer to speak at the program, but he also invited one of the team's current players to speak as well.

Sometimes finding a professional athlete is unnecessary. It may be easier, and as worthwhile, to invite amateur players and coaches from the community to speak to the students about their sport. Many amateurs are passionate about their favorite pastime and would make fine, enthusiastic presenters.

Often, amateur athletes belong to local sports clubs, which include popular and specialized sports. You may as easily find a club for polo or kayaking as you would for bicycling, volleyball, skiing, tennis, swimming, or sailing.

Cultural arts organizations frequently promote music, dance, and theater to children. If you live in or near a major city, consider what the symphony, opera, theater or ballet can offer. Frequently, these organizations advertise prepared programs directed toward elementary schools. For example, a symphony in Texas offers a 30-minute demonstration entitled "Musical Instruments." Throughout the country, theater troupes perform dramatizations of children's classics. Whether booking a prepared presentation or gathering support for an original program, cultural arts organizations can prove invaluable.

Most occupations have corresponding organizations that promote professional development. Their print resources and representatives could add markedly to a program. Because they probably participate in your district's career day events, guest speakers have developed fine presentations appropriate for children. Additionally, they may already have fine supplemental print material to share at your program. Keep in mind that your greatest support may come from professional organizations related to education and school library media centers. The American Library Association, International Reading Association, and National Education Association are a few of many outstanding organizations whose central purpose is to support your professional efforts. (see Photo 4.2)

Finally, consider sororities and fraternities for program support. Whether honorary or social, these groups often volunteer their time or resources for special community projects related to education.

Photo 4.2. Media specialist Pam Kanoy and students enjoy celebrating Dr. Seuss's Birthday, a special event sponsored by the National Education Association. *(Pilot Elementary School, Thomasville, North Carolina, Guilford County Schools)*

Figure 4.4 lists organizations that frequently support elementary schools and corresponding program titles.

Clubs and Organizations	Program Titles
Garden club	Designing a Garden
Symphony organization	Musical Instruments
Historical society	What Was (Your City) Like Fifty Years Ago?
Society for the Prevention of Cruelty to Animals (SPCA)	How to Care for Animals
Writer's club	How a Book is Made
Friends of public libraries	What Your Public Library Has to Offer You

Figure 4.4. Examples of organizations and clubs with program titles.

In addition to the organizations in Figure 4.4, consider:

cultural arts organizations (theater, ballet, opera, etc.)	hobby-related groups
sports clubs (tennis, ski, etc.)	fraternities and sororities
major sports organizations (NFL, NBA, etc.)	pet clubs
area sports organizations	professional organizations
political organizations	cultural groups
book clubs	various special interest organizations and clubs
medical-related charities and foundations	retired persons organizations

Government Agencies

National, state, and local government agencies have excellent materials and resource people for schools. Besides expert guest speakers, they have among the most extensive and reliable print resources for developing programs. Extra copies of their written material make great additions to the vertical file and reference section of school library media centers.

Foreign government agencies also share resources through their consulates and embassies. Frequently, their resources provide solid support for social studies programs and history reference material.

Government agencies frequently list their addresses and phone numbers in the front section of the telephone directory. To find them via the Internet, see the list of Web site addresses and detailed information about their content in Chapter 6. (Figure 4.5 lists some government agencies that support the elementary curriculum and corresponding program titles.)

U.S. Government Agencies	Program Titles
National Aeronautics and Space Administration	Aboard the Space Shuttle
Federal Aviation Agency	Highways in the Sky
U.S. Postal Service	What Happens to Your Letter
U.S. Department of Immigration & Naturalization	Becoming a Citizen
Federal Bureau of Investigation	Fingerprinting
National Parks Service	National Parks In Your State
Local Government Agencies	
Fire Department	How Fire Trucks Work
Police Department	How Police Cars Work
Municipal Court	A Day in Court
Mayor's Office (or City Manager)	What Your Mayor Does
Animal Control	Lost Animals
Parks and Recreation Department	Recreational Activities in Your City and Parks

Figure 4.5. Examples of government agencies and related program titles.

After exploring those agencies listed in Figure 4.5, consider the following government agencies that may have offices in large cities near the school:

United States Customs Service	Drug Enforcement Administration
Bureau of Indian Affairs	Branches of the military services
National Marine Fisheries Service	United States Congress
National Weather Service	United States Supreme Court
Department of Agriculture	Foreign consulates and embassies
United States Mint	Local government agencies

Media

Newspapers, television stations, radio stations, and magazines can help connect media specialists to resources. Pay special attention to local newspapers and Sunday supplements that include a section on "coming events," "happenings," or "what's going on in the community." These resources announce presentations by authors, scientists, actors, and sports stars. Movies and live dramatic productions of classics provide potential programming ideas. For example, one media specialist developed a program around Frances Burnett's classic, *The Secret Garden*. She encouraged students to read the book and view the movie version with their parents. Students who did both were then invited to a special program that included refreshments and a focused discussion contrasting the book and the movie.

Holiday and Special Event Organizers

When planning programs, capitalize on holidays and special events in the community. Halloween, Thanksgiving, Hanukkah, Christmas, and Valentine's Day provide familiar program topics. Holidays that honor special people, such as Columbus Day, Lincoln's Birthday, and Martin Luther King Jr. Day, can be springboards for programs relating to history and social studies. Many unique community events, like the hot-air balloon festival mentioned in Chapter 3, a fishing tournament, Mardi Gras, or an antique automobile show, can inspire program ideas. Contact event organizers to request materials and guest speakers for school library media programs.

Chamber of Commerce

The Chamber of Commerce has abundant information about local events. Each year, the members compile a community calendar listing holidays, meetings, celebrations, festivals, and other happenings. They are among the most informed and diverse resource connections you will find, and they can help at every stage of programming. Trying to decide on a relevant program topic? Consider offering a program that coincides with a community event listed on the calendar. Need help contacting local professionals? They can provide names, telephone numbers, and contact persons for nearby businesses as well as organizations and clubs. Having trouble finding a talented guest speaker? They can connect you to speakers' bureaus with experts on many special topics. Develop a positive rapport with the Chamber of Commerce. They are likely to be among your best program resources.

CONNECTING CONTENT AREAS WITH COMMUNITY RESOURCES

Community resources encompass so many possibilities that embarking on a search may overwhelm you. To narrow your search options, determine which community resources logically support different subject areas. Program theme can narrow your search even further. For programs supporting core curriculum, use the chart in Figure 4.6, below and on page 84.

Subject	Program Theme	Community Resource
Reading/ Language Arts	Author Visits	Authors (see Internet addresses in Chapter 6)
	Book Discussions (any book title)	Guests from community, parents, teachers
	Movie Discussions (any movie title)	Guests from community, parents, teachers, media
	Editing	Journal or book editor from university, media, parents
	Writing Stories	Writer's club in community
	Puppet Show	Guest from community who makes puppets (demonstration, displays)
	Read Alouds in Media Center	Parents, "Grandparents" Program, Principal
	Storytelling	Guest from community, parents, "Grandparents" Program, storytelling organization

Figure 4.6. Connecting content areas and community resources.

Figure 4.6—*Continued*

Subject	Program Theme	Community Resource
Social Studies	Travel Experience	Parents, teachers, guests from community, travel agent (slides and videos, displays, exhibits)
	Ethnic Foods (Food Festival)	Parents, guests from various cultures, chefs (demonstrations)
	Cultures of the World	Parents, guests from the community representing cultures (demonstrations, exhibits, displays, slides, videos)
	Government, Politics	Guests from local government, parents involved in topic
	Life During an Earlier Time Period	Grandparents/others describe growing up in earlier years (videos, movies, exhibits)
	Crafts from Pioneer Days	Grandparents, parents, guests from the community (exhibits, displays, demonstrations)
Science	Animals	Zoo mobile visits school; docent discusses animals with students
	Space	Speaker recommended by NASA visits media center
	Aviation	Military pilot visits media center and discusses history of aviation
	Oceanography	Film from district level library on sea life
	Ecology	Parent involved in environmental education visits media center
	Fish	Establish an aquarium interest center in media center; guest speaker visits to discuss the various types of fish in the aquarium

CONCLUSION

Almost any educational resource, whether purchased, rented, or made, can support programming. Identifying the most appropriate resources for your topic and audience gives your search clarity. Knowing where to find these resources in your school, district, and community gives it direction. Armed with this information, you can quickly select effective and economical resources for your program.

Chapter 5

How to Gather and Organize Resources

When doing research, navigating the electronic catalog and finding possible resources only begins the process. You must also know how to use available materials. Similarly, knowing where to find program resources is only a first step. Next, you must learn how to select the best resources. For example, choosing an outstanding speaker for a program would demand far different skills than finding an appropriate video clip, or ordering an exhibit from a museum. Different resources require different approaches.

SELECTING VOLUNTEERS

When selecting resources, consider the people most easily accessible to the school: parents, students, and teachers. All can be helpful volunteers with knowledge related to curriculum or student interests. To choose volunteers most suited to your program needs, gather data through surveys or questionnaires.

Parents

Many parents are eager to help at their child's school but cannot make long-term volunteer commitments. However, they might be available to speak or help at a single school library media program. As speakers, they can share professional experiences, leisure activities, travel adventures, or expertise on their favorite topics. Some may give fine demonstrations or make impressive media presentations. Even parents unable to share their time can contribute to the program by providing materials for displays or exhibits.

You can easily gather information on parents' interests and expertise by sending them surveys at the beginning of the year. First, meet with your principal to request permission to distribute the surveys. To make the most of this meeting:

- Begin by summarizing your plans for school library media programs.

- Describe the need for program resources.

- Explain the reasons for sending the survey.

- Discuss the benefits (to students, faculty, and you) of using parents as resources.

- Share a copy of the survey and letter that you will send to parents.

After securing the principal's permission, stress to teachers the far-reaching value of your survey. Explain that you will organize and file the surveys, then make them available for their use. Then ask them to help get the surveys out to parents through the children. (Figure 5.1 illustrates a survey that can be sent to parents.)

Survey results identify parents' specific knowledge, skills, unique possessions, non-print materials, and hobbies. They also indicate in what capacity each parent is able to volunteer. Regardless of the survey format, request several ways to contact parents. Beyond this requirement, library media specialists should mold the survey to fit the programming needs of their particular facility.

Students

Sometimes the surveys you send to parents may mention a son's or daughter's collections and special hobbies. More often, you will discover students' interests just by interacting with them. Instead of just indulging a child day after day by listening politely as he or she talks incessantly about a favorite pastime, recognize the program potential of that subject.

Because a child's fascination with a topic can be contagious, some students make fine guest speakers. Imagine giving *Peanuts* character Schroeder five minutes to tell classmates about Beethoven. Although Schroeder's topic might not interest his peers, some students become experts on subjects their classmates would love. Find an expert on a book, toy, computer program, video game, animal, insect, comic book character, real-life hero, almost any topic, and you can have an inspired program. Although students may not have much public speaking experience, their enthusiasm and knowledge can often captivate an audience. With a little coaching on how to streamline their presentation, students may become primary contributors to your most riveting programs.

Dear Parents:

Our school library media center is gathering ideas for special programs to offer as a means of supporting and enriching curriculum. If you have a hobby, special talent, skill, interest, or travel experience that you would like to share, please complete the survey below, and return it to your child's teacher.

Thank you,

Ann Kit
Library Media Specialist

- -

Date _____

COMMUNITY RESOURCES QUESTIONNAIRE

_____ Yes, I would like to share information/materials with the children at Benson Elementary.

Name _____ Phone _____

Name(s) of Children   Name(s) of Teacher(s)

_____   _____

_____   _____

Special Hobbies/Crafts:
     Description of Hobby/Craft: _____
     _____ I would be willing to discuss it with students.
     _____ I would be willing to demonstrate it.
     _____ I would be willing to share it with children as an exhibit.

Special Talents/Skills:
     Description of Talent/Skill: _____
     _____ I would be willing to discuss it with students.
     _____ I would be willing to demonstrate it.
     _____ I would be willing to contribute materials for a display.
     _____ I would be willing to share my storytelling ability with students.

Travel Experiences:
     Description (places): _____
     _____ I would like to discuss it with students.
     _____ I have slides, films, or photographs to share with students.
     _____ I have interesting materials from this country to contribute to a display.

Figure 5.1. Community resources questionnaire for parents.

Teachers

After gathering survey data, enter all relevant information into a community resources file. (Details for establishing the community resources file are provided in the next section.) Then make the file available to teachers. Also, foster a positive rapport with your colleagues by repaying them for helping distribute the surveys. As you learn about teachers' lessons, special projects, and classroom programs, flip through your files to find possible volunteers. A brief note or verbal tip about potential parent support can be invaluable to teachers. Even if you don't have specific recommendations, occasionally remind colleagues that your files are available for their perusal.

Finally, consider teachers as another program resource. Many departments are filled with outstanding teaching materials that enhance programming. Even though teachers are already overworked, some get rejuvenated by sharing a special skill and interest not related to their curriculum. To discover their interests, give teachers a survey similar to Figure 5.1. Encourage them to record hobbies, collections, travel experiences, and skills they might present to students.

The teachers' survey promises three other benefits. It makes teachers more aware of what the school library media center has to offer their students. It encourages them to look for possible resources to add to the file. It adds teacher recommendations to your list of program resources.

MAKING IT WORK WITH VOLUNTEERS

Recruiting and working with volunteers is essential for programming. Usually, parents help plan, prepare, and present programs. At other times, they fulfill regular media center duties while you and other volunteers work on special programs. Some prefer to share their skills and talents by volunteering as guest speakers. In any role, they are a valuable resource whose support should not be underestimated.

Parent volunteers can also help you develop a community resources file. After generating a set of questions for potential community resources, ask parent volunteers to make the telephone contacts. After these volunteers record their information, another can be in charge of developing and updating the resources file.

Prepare for Volunteers

To gather a parent volunteer team, you must know the district policy on obtaining volunteers. In some districts, policies are open-ended, leaving decisions to campus administrators. Others specify exact requirements for who may have volunteers, how many they may recruit, how they can be acquired, and how they should be assessed throughout the year. Whether strict or flexible, most districts have set rules about bringing volunteers into the building. In this era of heightened security concerns, follow the district or campus guidelines to the letter. In those rare cases where a written policy is not already in place, suggest creating one with the campus site-based committee or the faculty at large.

No matter what the circumstance, secure the principal's permission for whatever you do. It may take a dash of diplomacy and more than one meeting to convince the principal that you even need volunteers. Be persuasive and persistent. Even if you have support staff, volunteers are integral to program success.

After receiving permission to recruit or add more volunteers, keep the principal abreast of every stage of your volunteer program. Share a copy of the Volunteer Form (Figure 5.2, page 92). Update the principal on successes you owe to volunteer support. Most important, introduce parent volunteers to the principal (and his or her secretary) when they first begin working, then invite the principal to the library media center occasionally to see how much the volunteers are contributing to the school.

Recruit Volunteers

Simple forms are often the most successful recruiting tools. Succinct, direct requests set a professional tone. Parents who volunteer regularly will respect your efficiency. Though they work for free, they want their volunteer time to be productive. Parents who have never volunteered nor worked in a modern school library media center may be apprehensive. Well written request forms make good impressions. (see Figure 5.3, page 93) If they alone don't inspire cooperation, the information they provide may lead to future interactions that will.

Dear Parents:

Our school library media center needs your help. To keep the media center functioning at maximum potential, we depend on parent volunteers who make it possible to carry out unique activities and programs. Would you be willing to work in the school library media center several hours per week? If not, could you help us by performing some duties at home? Please complete the following questionnaire if you are interested in volunteering in any capacity. Your consideration is greatly appreciated.

LIBRARY MEDIA CENTER
VOLUNTEER FORM

Name: _____

Address: _____

_____

Phone: _____

E-mail: _____

Days and Times Available to work in LMC:

_____

_____

_____

Name(s) of Child(ren):

_____

_____

_____

Teacher(s):

_____

_____

_____

Special Skills/Talents/Interests:

_____ Word Processing   _____ Artwork/Graphics

_____ Internet Research   _____ Laminating

_____ Read Aloud   _____ Filing

_____ Storytelling   _____ Book Repair

Other types of work you enjoy: _____

_____

_____

Figure 5.2 Volunteer recruitment form for parents.

VOLUNTEER TASK REQUEST

Volunteer's Name: _____

Phone: _____

e-mail: _____

Days and Times Available: _____

Please check the library media center tasks that interest you:

_____ Word Processing

_____ Working at circulation desk

_____ Laminating

_____ Helping to process books

_____ Helping to develop learning centers

_____ Contacting resources and recording information in resources file

_____ Repairing damaged books

_____ Shelving books

_____ Reading stories aloud

_____ Storytelling

_____ Processing audio visual materials

_____ Maintaining vertical file

_____ Supervising reference area

_____ Assisting with displays and exhibits

_____ Filing cards

_____ Internet searches

Figure 5.3 Volunteer task request (to be given to volunteers after orientation).

CONTACTING RESOURCES

Although you will set your own program goals and make all final decisions about program content, you may delegate many other responsibilities to volunteers. Contacting resource people and organizing the contact information may not be difficult, but it is important. Good programs need good contact people and material resources. Finding them and accessing information about them requires communication and organization skills.

List Possible Resources

Prepare your volunteers for contacting possible resources. Begin by describing your program goals and the resources you think can support it. Then discuss with your volunteers the campus, district, and community resources listed in Chapter 4. Help your volunteers begin their searches. Guide them to references that initiate their searches. District contact lists, local telephone directories, and Internet search engines can all be fine starting points for locating resources. Be available to answer questions or offer help, but trust that your volunteers can handle the task alone. This process is not difficult. It just takes time, persistence, and tenacity.

Interview Potential Resources

After your volunteers have a list of contacts, they can begin conducting telephone interviews to determine what program support that contact can provide. Suggest that volunteers keep the interview succinct. They should begin by introducing themselves, then explaining that they have called to gain program support. Immediately after, volunteers should ask predetermined questions like those listed below. Whenever possible, have them tailor questions to the goals of a particular program.

1. Are you interested in sharing information concerning your field of expertise, skills, or area of interest with elementary students?

2. Where are you (or your business) located?

3. Are you willing to visit (or send people from your business) to our school?

4. What would you (or your business) like to offer students?

5. Do you think you can relate the information to elementary students?

6.   Will you need computer or audiovisual equipment?

7.   What is the length of time needed for the program?

8.   Are there certain days that you are available?

9.   How much notice do you require?

10   Could you supply any handouts to the students?

11.   Would you be able to provide materials for a display or exhibit?

12.   What types of information will you share during the presentation?

13.   Do you know a teacher or parent at this school?

During the interview, the volunteers should record information in an organized manner. After asking the predetermined questions, they can request brochures or pamphlets that provide more information. Finally, the volunteer should thank the contact person, but leave the final statement open-ended. They may say, "Thank you for your time. I will share this information with the media specialist." Or, "Thank you for sharing this information. You've been very helpful." Be sure volunteers do not state or imply that someone will call back. Even if the contact seems promising, you may find a better, more convenient, or less expensive resource. Or, you may end up changing your program plans. Leave your options open, and do not let volunteers create expectations of you that you may not be able to fulfill.

After their telephone interview, review the information and, if necessary, discuss that contact person further with the volunteer. Primarily, decide if the information on this contact is worth recording for future use. Based on curricular needs and student interests, is this person or business a good potential resource for future programs? If the answer is yes, then record the information onto the community resources card. Over time, the resource cards, brochures, and pamphlets will need to be organized for easy access.

ORGANIZING
THE RESOURCES

Organize your resources using whatever method makes sense to you. Through her rodeo program, Sue Wiley discovered the value of putting her materials in order.

As I began to assemble all the information for my program, I quickly realized how things were getting out of hand. Soon files of information began getting scattered. I had some by my phone, some on the work room table, and some beside the materials that teachers were bringing for the program. Over several days, I discovered that I was spending most of my preparation time looking for files that I had set down when distracted.

Finally, I stopped doing anything on the program and just spent one afternoon creating a file box of all the information I had collected from the beginning of the planning process. Once I had some modicum of order to things, preparing my program became much more efficient. That day, I determined to organize all my materials after my event was over so next year I could put my hands on anything I needed as soon as I needed it.

Like Sue, media specialists know that organization is synonymous with efficiency. Therefore, after identifying and contacting resources from the community, organize the resources for maximum use. Both a community resources file and a vertical file can help.

Establish a Community Resources File

Creating a community resources file for the campus or district is worthwhile for all types of program development, including special programs initiated by teachers and administrators. Place resource data into a separate file drawer organized in whatever way seems most appropriate. Some media specialists like a straightforward alphabetized arrangement of all resources. Others organize them by the different types of resources identified in Chapter 4. Still others file resources according to the programs for which they were used.

Include Resources in a Vertical File

Rather than keeping a separate resources file, you may find it more efficient to store resource data with other program materials. Background information, notes on modifications for next year, student art, and lists of resource people and materials can be stored in one file pocket for easy access. When the program is repeated, you will find everything for the program stored in one place.

No matter what the preferred method of organization, inform grade-level teams or individual classroom teachers about the location and organization of program resources. Not only will this help them find materials when they plan a unit, but it also enables them to contribute more resources to the library media center when they find something not already included in the file.

Establishing a community resources file and/or vertical file for a school seems like an overwhelming task, but it does not have to be. After making the commitment to develop such a file, lighten the load by assigning the work to parent volunteers. To start the process, implement the following steps.

Select an Interested Parent Volunteer(s)

When establishing the file, brainstorm with parent volunteers and teachers. Devise a systematic plan to develop the file. Then recruit a volunteer who enjoys projects involving organization and who can see the job through to completion. Usually by discussing the project with volunteers, some will be genuinely interested. It is best if only one or two volunteers tackle the project; that way, they can better claim "ownership" of the work. The volunteers can pursue the project in the school library media center once a week. If they need more time, you can suggest they work on the project at home.

Determine the Best Format

Sometimes consistency makes finding resources easy. Consequently, some media specialists organize everything using the exact same format. Others look at the materials they must organize, and determine the easiest way to store it and then access it again in the future. Whatever format you choose, keep it simple. Teachers should be able to search through them without needing your help. The most common formats include:

1. Folder format. Folders are arranged alphabetically by topic in a filing cabinet, much like a vertical file. In each folder, store flyers, pamphlets, handouts, photos, as well as information about the community resource. (See Figure 5.4, page 98, for a community resources sample form.)

2. Catalog card format. Record all information on a single, small card, and include a notation about where to find related materials. (see Figure 5.5, page 99)

3. Larger card (usually 4 x 6) format. Record information on the cards arranged in an appropriate sized file box. Store the box near materials associated with the program.

4. Electronic format. If you use an online catalog that uses standard MARC format, then you may wish to incorporate community resources information into the MARC format designed specifically for community resources. If you do not have an online catalog, you can develop your own community resources database using one of the database management programs.

COMMUNITY RESOURCES FORM

_____   _____
                Topic   Date

Name _____

Contact Person _____

Address _____

_____

Phone _____   Fax _____

e-mail Address _____

Type of Program _____

Grade Levels _____

Length of Time Required _____

Equipment Needs _____

Availability _____

Fees _____

Program Description _____

_____

_____

_____

_____

Comments_____

_____

_____

_____

_____

Date of Entry_____

Figure 5.4. Sample form for community resources file folder.

Topic _____   Date _____

Name _____   Grade Levels _____

Address _____   Availability _____

_____   Equipment Needs _____

Phone _____   _____

Fax _____   Fee _____

e-mail _____

Description _____

Comments _____

_____

_____

_____

Figure. 5.5. Sample card for community resources file.

Determine What the File Should Contain

Regardless of the format you choose, record the following information on each card about every resource:

- Name of person, business, company, institution, club, agency
- Street and e-mail address
- Fax and phone number
- Time available
- Length of program
- Special audiovisual equipment needs
- Appropriate target group to which the resource will appeal (age, grade, etc.)
- Fees (if any)

- General program description
- Date of entry

Also include a brief evaluation of the resource after using it. For example, after a program with a guest speaker, record personal observations and feedback from teachers and students on the reverse side of the form or card.

Determine File Arrangement

Arranging the file is important especially if it will be used by faculty, staff, and administrators. Some arrangements to consider:

- Arrange alphabetically by name of person or business
- Arrange alphabetically by topic to which that resource contributes
- Cross-reference by name and topic

Determine Who May Use the File

It is best to make the community resources file available to all faculty at your school, administrators and other media specialists in the district, and in some cases, students working on projects. When school library media specialists and the local public library staff work together and share files, patrons of both benefit, and the work of maintaining a file is easier to justify. By sharing, both parties have access to more resources.

Because so few media specialists have a community resources file, some industrious media specialists join together to establish one file to be shared between campuses. Thanks to the common practice of interlibrary loan, even students are familiar with the concept of shared resources.

Publicize the Availability of the File

For the file to be used, you must advertise its availability to teachers, the principal, parents, students, and others in the district. Share your rationale for developing the file and remind them that its existence enhances programs in the classroom, at grade levels, and throughout the entire school. Not only will the file help you develop programs, but it also encourages teachers to begin programming as well. Even if they never use the file for anything else, teachers will be grateful to you for providing access to guest speakers.

Revise the File Regularly

Determine a policy for updating the file and add it to the formal school library media center policy manual. Updates of the community resources file are necessary. Yet, as most library media specialists know, this task is much like the weeding process. Although the work is not difficult, finding time to do it may be a challenge. Therefore, assign the job of keeping up with the community resources file to one or two volunteers who enjoy this type of work. Let them be responsible for deleting inaccurate or outdated contact information as well as adding new or updated data. Verifying the information every year or two will ensure easy contact when you need it.

CONCLUSION

Clearly, library media specialists who know how to find, gather, and organize resources are well equipped to put together dynamic programs. Knowledge of the resources both within and beyond the community can support programming in the most vital way. It transforms an ordinary, predictable program into a riveting event rich in content and extended learning.

Chapter 6

Searching the Internet for Community Resources

The Internet's expansiveness and rapid growth afford previously unimaginable access to information. However, this benefit gives rise to two concerns: Web sites can come and go very quickly, and all Web sites require the discerning eye of educators to ensure that the information given is accurate. Taking these two concerns into consideration, we have compiled a list of outstanding Web sites that will support library programming.

Each Web site corresponds to the community resources discussed in Chapter 4 or relates to personal interests and popular children's authors and illustrators. Some sites were created expressly for educators. Others include Web pages targeted to children. No matter what their format or purpose, every Web site contains valuable information for media specialists, teachers, and students.

Sites indicated with an asterisk [*] offer excellent starting points, as they provide links to numerous other resources related to the specific category. All sites listed support programming in the following ways:

1. You may gather ideas to plan and develop programs.

2. You may gain more information on the program topic.

3. You may use them to locate resources, including people, exhibits, activities, pamphlets, and other supplemental resources.

4. Teachers may acquire information and activities to prepare students for upcoming programs.

5. Students may access the Web sites to research a program topic, participate in online activities, or take virtual field trips to extend and reinforce learning.

BUSINESS AND INDUSTRY

Web sites for businesses and corporations abound. Knowing where to find listings of businesses within your community and across the United States can speed your planning stages considerably. In addition to providing extensive information, business and industry offer excellent resources for finding guest speakers, supplemental material, and even financial support for programming.

BigYellow
   http://www.bigyellow.com/
This site lists businesses by category or state and has educational links to reference sources and resources for teachers.

* *Guide to the Web*
   http://www.theactgroup.com/telephon.htm
This extensive site contains the following sections that will provide media specialists access to various resources:

Switchboard—nationwide telephone and address directory

InfoSpace—personal, business and government phone, fax and e-mail

Anywho—AT&T's clear directory also includes a reverse directory

Zip2 Yellow Pages—search businesses by name, category, or distance from home

Directory of toll free numbers from Infospace—quick access to toll free numbers

Big Yellow—national business yellow pages and residential listings from NYNEX

Thomas Register of Manufacturers—the most complete list of manufacturers

WhoWhere—an e-mail address database

Zip Code and Zip + 4 Finder—a simple and efficient zip code directory

Smartpages.com
   http://http1.smartpages.com/
This online directory of business listings and city and shopping guides is designed to help consumers shop, research products and services, locate merchants and plan entertainment, leisure and travel activities.

GOVERNMENT AGENCIES

Many government agencies have Web sites that can enrich library programs. Some sites include pages specifically designed for educators. Access these sites to research a program topic, develop program ideas, gather resources, and plan activities.

Gradually, these sites have added components directed to children. As a result, you might also encourage students to visit some sites before or after attending your program to learn more about the topic. Children will enjoy exploring the topic and participating in the entertaining activities.

Also, note that many government sites include areas for teachers and parents. Some even contain virtual tours and online libraries that provide maps, photographs, and other helpful resources.

Special Government Sites for Educators

Louisiana State University. "A List of Federal Agencies on the Internet"
   http://www.lib.lsu.edu/gov/exec.html.
   Maintained by Louisiana State University, this site lists all the U.S. federal government agencies on the Internet and links them to their sites. It has two main divisions: (1) Executive Branch and Agencies, and (2) Independent Establishments and Government Corporations. Subheadings for each are the same and include Judicial; Legislative; Independent; Boards, Commissions, and Committees; Quasi-Official; and Complete U.S. Federal Government Agencies Directory.

National Aeronautics and Space Administration (NASA) Education Program
   http://education.nasa.gov/
   Linked to *A Guide to NASA's Education Programs*, this searchable database contains brief descriptions of NASA's education programs, including points of contact, admission criteria, location, content areas, and financial support for all of NASA's field centers. Visitors can access a variety of educational programs, materials and services. Here you will find contact information and resources arranged by NASA field centers, states, and regions throughout the United States.

National Archives and Records Administration. "The Digital Classroom"
   http://www.nara.gov/education/classrm.html
   To encourage teachers at all levels to use archival documents in the classroom, the "Digital Classroom" shares materials from the National Archives and methods for teaching with primary sources.

National Park Service
http://www.nps.gov/
This central hub for almost all of the 375 sites found in the National Park System connects educators to numerous sites focusing on "America's natural and cultural heritage through the National Parks." Web pages range from publications, video presentations, and guided walks and talks to extensive curriculum-based education programs.

Special Government Sites for Children

Air Force: Air Force Link, Jr.
http://www.af.mil/aflinkjr/
This is a game room containing 10 activities, a media lab, an air field, and a post office that all teach about the Air Force. Fun activities include instructions for making a delta wing or a broad wing paper airplane, and directions for sending a friend an online Air Force postcard. The other branches of the military also offer their own sites.

CIA's Homepage for Kids
http://www.odci.gov/cia/ciakids/index.html
This interactive and fun-filled site explains the functions and background of the CIA. It also offers a virtual tour of the CIA. Students will particularly enjoy the "CIA Canine Corp," "Try a Disguise," and the "CIA Exhibit Center."

Department of Health and Human Services
http://www.hhs.gov/families/kids.htm
This site provides useful links to numerous other sites that contain information about different agencies in the federal government and activities especially for children. All of these sites, some of which are listed individually in this chapter, focus on teaching children about the agencies through activities and games.

FBI
http://www.fbi.gov/kids/kids.htm
Children learn about the FBI at this site which is divided into three visitor levels: kids (K-5), youth (6-12), and parent/teacher. A special DOJ (Department of Justice) kids' page teaches forensics, DNA and polygraph testing, and fingerprinting. In the areas such as "Working Dogs," "Crime Detection," "Crime Prevention," and "Junior Special Agent Program," youngsters learn about the different departments of the FBI.

Federal Emergency Management Agency (FEMA)
http://www.fema.gov/kids
Here, children can learn, play games, and read stories about the different types of disasters, including tornadoes, earthquakes, and hurricanes. Visitors who follow the tornado can become a FEMA "Disaster Action Kid" and get a certificate from FEMA. Disaster Action Kids also get to be a part of a special e-mail group that receives exciting news and information directly from FEMA on a regular basis. In addition to general weather information, this site teaches safety tips, including a section that helps families prepare for disaster.

National Highway Traffic Safety Administration (NHTSA)
http://www.nhtsa.dot.gov/kids/
Join Larry and Vince, NHTSA's crash test dummies, for a tour of the hot spots around town and learn about traffic safety. Visit the "Safety School" and "Larry's Art Gallery." Lesson plans and materials related to safety are available at this fun-filled, interactive site.

National Institute of Environmental Health Sciences (NIEHS)
http://www.niehs.nih.gov/kids/home.htm
Numerous links to "hot topics" related to environmental health sciences, games such as word scrambles, spelling bees, and a sing-along section (complete with sound) make learning about environmental health sciences entertaining and informative.

U.S. Department of Energy
http://www.scied.science.doe.gov
Children and educators will enjoy visiting this site to learn more about science, technology, energy, engineering, and math. Interesting and fun-filled activities enrich the learning experience.

U.S. Department of Treasury
http://www.ustreas.gov/kids/
Youngsters can find information about savings bonds, learn about taxes with a lemonade stand example, and sign up for games and resources. A favorite area is the "U.S. Mint" which shares basic information about how money is minted.

White House for Kids
http://www.whitehouse.gov/WH/kids/html/home.html
Visit the White House on this popular site designed for "helping young people become more active and informed citizens." Viewers can learn about the location and history of the White House, our presidents, and their children. The history area provides links to presidents and first ladies of the past, and viewers are encouraged to send mail to the president, vice president, and their spouses.

Other Recommended Sites

Federal Highway Administration
> **http://www.fhwa.dot.gov/education/k-5home.htm**

Federal Transit Association
> **http://www.fta.dot.gov/transcity**

Social Security Administration
> **http://www.ssa.gov/kids/index.htm**

U.S. Department of Justice
> **http://www.usdoj.gov/kidspage/**

U.S. Department of the Interior
> **http://www.doi.gov/kids/**

U.S. Environmental Protection Agency
> **http://www.epa.gov/kids**

U.S. Geological Survey
> **http://www.usgs.gov/education/**

U.S. State Department. "Digital Diplomacy for Students"
> **http://www.state.gov/www.digital_diplomacy/index.html**

INSTITUTIONS

Because many are directly linked to education, institutions are among the best resources to support programming. Rather than sharing only general information, many of these Web sites offer activities for children, interactive games, teacher resources, online libraries, and guide visitors through virtual tours of exhibits and galleries. When planning your program, take advantage of the extensive information most of these sites share on a variety of topics.

Aquariums

National Aquarium in Baltimore
> **http://www.aqua.org/**

Visitors are invited to dive into this Web site of fun information about animals, exhibits, conservation efforts, and the institution itself. Some interactive games are especially popular with youngsters.

UnderWater World
http://www.underwaterworld.com/
Visit UnderWater World at the Mall of America in Bloomington, Minnesota, and you can take a trip not only through, but also under the aquarium's exhibits: a Minnesota Lake, the Mississippi River, the Gulf of Mexico, and a Caribbean reef.

University of Hawaii. "The Waikiki Aquarium"
http://www.mic.hawaii.edu/aquarium
This outstanding site offers a beautiful virtual tour where users can click on any creature to gain information about it. The library area provides a searchable database of Web sites and resources about the aquarium, its exhibits, and Hawaiian and South Pacific marine life.

Libraries

Herbert Hoover Presidential Library and Museum
http://www.hoover.nara.gov/
When using the Internet for program enrichment, don't forget about the wealth of information that can be found at the presidential libraries. This site focuses on Herbert Hoover's entire life and accomplishments. "Just for Kids" is packed with interesting information and fun-filled activities. For example, the "Dear Laura" area encourages children to ask questions about Laura Ingalls Wilder and her pioneer days, and the staff will e-mail replies.

Library of Congress
http://lcweb.loc.gov/
Browse this huge site to become familiar with the plethora of information available to support media center programs. Overviews of the Library of Congress exhibitions are shared at the online gallery. The "Fun Site for Kids and Family" offers a variety of learning experiences. For example, "Meet Amazing Americans" presents photographs and detailed information about famous inventors, politicians, performers, and activists.

New York Public Library
http://www.nypl.org
This site has everything imaginable for library users: catalogs, a digital library collection, archival collections, health information, and electronic resources. "On Lion for Kids" is a highly recommended section that contains information about author and book characters, children's events, recommended readings, and games and activities.

Universities, Colleges, and Schools

*All About College
http://www.allaboutcollege.com/
At *All About College* you'll find thousands of links to colleges and universities around the world including admissions office e-mail addresses for most schools. The list includes colleges in the United States, Canada, Africa, Asia, Europe, Australia, Mexico, and South America.

*American School Directory
http://www.asd.com/
Want to see what's going on at other schools across the nation? Here you can access more than 70,000 school sites. By visiting the individual school sites, library media specialists can gain a wealth of exciting ideas related to special events, curriculum, and activities.

*American Universities and Colleges
http://www.globalcomputing.com/universy.html
This site provides a complete listing of universities and colleges that can be accessed by the name of the college or the state.

Museums

*Smithsonian Institution
http://www.si.edu/newstart.htm
This address takes you to the general information site of the Smithsonian Institution with links to its various museums and galleries, zoos, and research facilities. Each of these areas has its own Web site, with opportunities for excellent online tours, activities, and teacher information. The site also offers a useful alphabetical listing of subject areas to help organize the vast information available.

Photo 6.1 Following a special program, students search the Smithsonian Institution's Web site for more information. (*Edward White Elementary, El Lago, Texas, Clear Creek Independent School District*)

Air and Space

The International Women's Air and Space Museum
http://www.iwasm.org/
Like the museum now located at Burke Lakefront Airport in Dayton, Ohio, this site is dedicated to "preserving the history of women in aviation." Biographical information, photographs, and interesting facts about women who have made major contributions to aviation and space is available.

National Air and Space Museum
http://www.nasm.si.edu/nasm/edu/
This site contains information and activities about aviation and space topics such as the exploration of the universe. Be sure to explore the educational links, the online galleries, and the special area for teachers.

Art

*Yahooligans: Arts and Entertainment: Art: Museums and Galleries
http://www.yahooligans.com/Arts_and_Entertainment/Art /Museums_and_Galleries/
This excellent site links visitors to over 75 different museums and galleries including the Smithsonian, the Guggenheim Museum, and the Library of Congress: American Treasures. The listing is alphabetical and includes a brief description of the museum or gallery. Some of the outstanding art museum sites that can be accessed include:

Fine Arts Museum of San Francisco. **http://ww.thinker.org/**

Louvre Museum. **http://www.louvre.fr/louvrea.htm**

The Metropolitan Museum of Art. **http://www.metmuseum.org/**

National Gallery of Art. **http://www.nga.gov/home.htm**

Smithsonian Institution: National Museum of American Art. **http://www.nmaa.si.edu/**

Visitors to the above sites will discover virtual tours of galleries, in-depth looks at specific artists and works of art, and virtual tours of current or past exhibits. Many of these sites list services for teachers and schools, teaching resources, and information to use when visiting the galleries.

Children's

Children's Museum of Indianapolis
http://www.childrensmuseum.org/index2.htm
This well-designed museum site is packed with information for educators and students. "Fun On-Line" provides interesting science activities

and photographs (complete with sound) that will enrich any school library program. "Just for Teachers" offers field trip information, and the community resources database is particularly useful to library media specialists. Of special interest is the list of the educational materials available for Indiana educators to check out.

Hands On Children's Museum
http://www.hocm.org/
This Web site provides a description of the new exhibits at the museum in Olympia, Washington. Children from around the world make contributions to the area, "Kids' Jokes and Riddles." Educators and students will find the links to "cool sites" about science useful.

The New Chicago Children's Museum at Navy Pier
http://wkarch.com/ccm.htm
Visit the museum online and find out what it has to offer. The Web site includes photographs of the various areas of the museum and a description of the various exhibits.

History

National Museum of the American Indian
http://www.si.edu/nmai
The museum, located in Washington, D.C., highlights the history of the American Indian. The Web site provides detailed information concerning the various programs offered.

Smithsonian Institution. "National Museum of American History"
http://www.si.edu/info/education.htm
The well-designed virtual exhibits include a variety of topics such as "The American Presidency" and "Star-Spangled Banner." Special activities can be found in the "Not Just for Kids" area.

Science

American Museum of Natural History
http://www.amnh.org/
One of the world's finest museums located in New York City can be accessed online. You don't want to miss the virtual tours (complete with sound) of the museum's various exhibits. Be sure to visit "Ology," the museum's new Web site for kids, and browse the area specifically designed for educators.

Franklin Institute
http://sln.fi.edu
Take an online journey and learn about science topics and exhibits at this Philadelphia museum. Science educators and media specialists planning a science-related program will find links to Internet resources, games, puzzles, science activities, and lessons.

Museum of Science: Boston
http://www.mos.org/home.html
Viewers of this site can visit excellent online exhibits. For example, "The Virtual Fish Tank" turns your computer into an aquarium. Various activities, resources, and Web links make this an excellent resource for enriching science programs.

The Museum of Science, Art and Human Perception (San Francisco). "The Exploratorium"
http://www.exploratorium.edu/
Housed in San Francisco's Palace of Fine Arts, the Exploratorium is a "collage of 650 science, art, and human perception exhibits." These exhibits are highlighted at this site, and a digital library to 10,000 pages of the Exploratium Web site provides information on a vast array of topics.

Smithsonian Institution. "National Museum of Natural History"
http://www.mnh.si.edu/
This is another fine individual site developed by the Smithsonian Institution. The numerous topics highlighted at this site are packed with interesting information and photographs. Electronic field trips, educational resources, and exhibits make this site a top priority when developing library programs.

Zoos

Bronx Zoo
http://www.bronxzoo.com/
The Bronx Zoo in New York is home to more than 4,000 animals, including some of the world's most endangered species. Be sure to take an online tour of the zoo. For example, kids don't want to miss the "Congo Virtual Tour" where they meet the Congo residents and play a Congo game.

*Conservation Breeding Specialist Group: Global Zoo Directory
http://www.cbsg.org/gzd.htm
This comprehensive directory of zoos around the world provides links to various sites and information on the nature of each institution's collection.

London Zoo
http://www.zsl.org/londonzoo/index.html
Established in 1828 and open to the public since 1847, the London Zoo has long been one of the most famous zoos in the world. Visit this site and take a guided tour through the zoo, gather activities, and learn the latest news about the animal residents.

San Diego Zoo
http://www.sandiegozoo.org/
This interactive and information-packed site is a must. Learn facts about animals and zoos as you visit such spots as the "Virtual Photo Album." Photographs, videos, and interactive activities make this an excellent site for enriching library programs.

Smithsonian Institution. "National Zoo"
http://www.si.edu/natzoo
At this Smithsonian Institution site, see the animals up close with the zoo's "Wild Webcams." On ZooTV you can see elephants, flamingoes, kiwis, and more. The animal video library allows an online view of the zoo's exhibits.

CLUBS AND ORGANIZATIONS

For programs related to students' personal interests, search Web sites developed by clubs and organizations. Occasionally sites related to professional interests and careers may be helpful. But because so many sites target children's personal interests exclusively, your challenge will likely be in narrowing the number of hits for any topic. Especially helpful are sites about children's clubs, sports organizations, and hobbies and collectibles.

Children's Clubs

Boys & Girls Clubs
http://www.bgca.org/html/home.html
The site shares stories about special young people and programs, links users to other sites such as *Read Across America*, and provides information about an after-school program called "Kids Can Do." The best area of the site is "Tour the Club," a look at the inside of a club. When viewers click on the floor plan to visit the club entry, gymnasium, arts and crafts room, game room, or learning/tech center, they see photos of the area with a brief description of its background and purpose.

Boys Scouts of America
http://www.bsa.scouting.org/

Sign up for scouting at this informative site. Background information on the Boy Scouts of America, educational games, quizzes, and interactive resources are available.

Camp Fire Boys and Girls
http://www.campfire.org/
News releases and information about local Camp Fire groups, fundraising, and volunteer opportunities are available at this site. "About Camp Fire Boys and Girls" links visitors to the various programs of the organization.

Girl Scouts
http://www.gsusa.org/
Although this excellent site is primarily designed for participants in the Girl Scout program, it also offers great links for all girls. In addition to the local scouting information, volunteer opportunities, and organizational information, the site presents "Just 4 Girls" filled with activities and other links including viewer subscriptions of poetry, artwork, and literature; a chat room; exploration of careers; and much more.

Sports Organizations

Major League Baseball
http://www.majorleaguebaseball.com/
Baseball news, special features, statistics, standings, schedules, and information about players can be found at this popular site. While here, visitors may want to listen to a live game on audio or view one on video.

NASCAR
http://www.nascar.com/
This site provides news, race results, schedules, standings, and team information about NASCAR. A store is also available to visitors.

National Archery Association
http://www.usarchery.org/
This site, developed by the National Governing Body for U.S. Olympic Archery, provides a calendar of events and programs on how to train for the sport and qualify for competitions.

National Basketball Association
http://www.nba.com/
News releases, special features, statistics, team schedules, and the NBA store are available online. Students will also enjoy viewing information about the players and the history of basketball.

National Football League
> **http://www.nfl.com/**

This popular site contains news, statistics, and team standings as well as information about the players. The special area designed for kids offers football facts, games, and interesting activities. The "QB Club" and "Coaches Club" allow visitors to chat online with quarterbacks and coaches.

U.S. Figure Skating
> **http://www.usfsa.org/**

Visit this site for news and information about figure skating events, the athletes, and contest results. Links make up the bulk of this site. "Clubs" lists USFSA clubs around the United States and "Synch" focuses on synchronized team skating.

U.S. Soccer
> **http://www.us-soccer.com/**

This official Web site of the U.S. Soccer Federation contains sections on media, publications, national teams, members, coaching and referees.

Hobbies and Collectibles

American Philatelic Society
> **http://www.stamps.org/**

Stamp collectors will enjoy this engaging site that also provides a special area "Just For Kids."

Antiques Roadshow Jr.
> **http://www.pbs.org/wgbh/pages/roadshow/series /jrroadshow/aboutoverview.html**

This site is devoted to the interests of young collectors and their families.

Beanie Babies
> **http://www.beaniebabies.com/**

The official site of Beanie Babies is one of the most popular with children. Visitors can search for favorite Beanie Baby friends, see their photographs, and determine if they are retired. Games and activities are also provided.

Coin-Gallery Online
> **http://www.coin-gallery.com/**

Information about coin collecting, major coin shows, exciting exhibits, and much more can be found at this interesting site. An educational resources area is also provided.

VIRTUAL FIELD TRIPS

Although many sites previously listed include virtual field trips, a few more deserve mentioning. These Web sites prepare students for upcoming programs or reinforce learning afterward. Nearly every site includes special activities worth exploring.

GOAL—Global Online Adventure Learning Site, Inc.
http://www.goals.com/homebody.asp
GOAL provides educational adventures in science, technology, and nature. Adventures include a family voyage aboard a sailboat in the Pacific, a world tour using only human power, and a voyage to circumnavigate the world using oar power.

Passport to Knowledge
http://www.passporttoknowledge.com/
This outstanding site, supported by organizations such as National Science Foundation, NASA, and public television, contains "interactive learning experiences using space-age telecommunications to connect students and teachers with our planet's leading researchers." The site encourages educators to move beyond the textbook and excite students about science by providing such activities as "Passport to Antarctica" and "Passport to the Rainforest." Online discussion groups, teacher support groups, and teacher resources are also provided.

Rice University's Virtual Tour. "Glacier"
http://www.glacier.rice.edu
Rice University sponsors this virtual visit to Antarctica developed by a graduate student, a polar explorer, and a high school teacher with goals to create a Web site and develop "hands-on, inquiry based, thematic curriculum" for teachers and students. The site provides information and photographs of the region and its inhabitants.

The Virtual Field Trips Site
http://www.field-guides.com/
The virtual trips at this site are really tours through different Web sites to learn about subjects like deserts, hurricanes, oceans, and volcanoes. Each field trip includes detailed lesson plans with terms and concepts to learn before the trip, and other classroom resources.

Yahoo! Recreation: Travel: Virtual Field Trips
http://dir.yahoo.com/recreation/travel/
This site provides more than twenty virtual field trips including a bike journey in Africa, an archaeological excavation in Egypt, and Arctic adventures in Greenland.

CHILDREN'S AUTHORS AND ILLUSTRATORS

When preparing for an author visit or creating an author-related interest center, you are no longer limited to reference books. The Internet contains a wealth of information about the personal lives and professional achievements of children's authors and illustrators. Some sites include photographs, bibliographies, awards and achievements, and learning activities related to specific books. For educators, they often provide information about scheduling author visits and ordering resources. For students, they include answers to frequently asked questions, and some provide an opportunity for students to correspond with authors by e-mail.

Children's Literature Web Guide
http://www.acs.ucalgary.ca/~dkbrown/authors.html
This Web site is a good starting point when researching children's authors and illustrators. The site provides links to a multitude of sites for authors and illustrators. Many of the best sites are maintained by publishers.

Tedd Arnold
http://www.geocities.com/~teddarnold/
Trying to find information about Arnold's life and works? This colorful, entertaining site presents biographical information, questions from kids, a schedule of author appearances, and book information. Tedd Arnold provides a detailed step-by-step look at how he illustrates and describes his work in progress.

Jan Brett
http://www.janbrett.com/
At this popular Web site you will find basic information about Brett's books, tour appearances, and personal life as well as wonderful activities for students and media specialists. The well-designed site offers contests with entries posted on the Web, a monthly audio message (a Hedge-a-gram) from Jan Brett, artwork, and activities such as designing character masks.

Public Broadcasting System. "Marc Brown"
>http://www.pbs.org/wgbh/arthur/

Meet the "Arthur" book characters on the Internet and have fun learning about the author of these popular books. Teachers' guides, parent information, librarian information, and much more can be found. The "Librarians Nook" includes educational activities, a script for the play, "D.W. Gets Her Library Card," and a description of all related television episodes, books, videos, CDs, and audiocassettes.

Betsy Byars
>http://www.betsybyars.com/

The best feature of this site is "Writing Tips," a special personal essay by Betsy Byars who offers practical advice for writing. She begins with, "That's my first tip—read!" The site also includes biographical information, questions and answers, a book list, and a beautiful photo album of Betsy's past.

Eric Carle
>http://www.eric-carle.com/

Packed with interesting information, this popular site shares biographical information about Eric Carle and highlights his beautiful picture books. The best feature is the "Caterpillar Express," a newsletter from Eric Carle. He warmly answers the questions that he is most often asked such as: "Why do you use small creatures in your books most of the time? What is your favorite color? Do you have any hobbies? When did you grow a beard?"

Tomie dePaola
>http://www.bingley.com

This site contains photographs and information about dePaola's life, works, and awards. It also shares valuable resources and the answers to frequently asked questions. A schedule of his appearances is provided, and links to Penguin Books provide opportunities for author visits.

Mem Fox
>http://www.memfox.net/

This unique Web site is organized like a book with chapters and a contents page. The chapters include "All About Mem," "Mem's Books," "For Parents and Teachers," "For Writers and Potential Writers," and "Mem's Guestbook."

Jean Craighead George
>http://www.jeancraigheadgeorge.com/

Learn more about George's life and books through an extensive question–and–answer section. There are also numerous photographs of the author from childhood to adulthood. Audio and video clips are available.

Katherine Paterson
http://www.terabithia.com/

Paterson's Web site contains author information that is presented in a unique way through an Internet interview using questions asked by children and educators from a New York elementary school. A list of her works, awards, and a schedule of upcoming events are also presented.

Patricia Polacco
http://www.patriciapolacco.com/

Polacco shares her books and her life by showing photographs of her house and studio and providing information about her background, family, and work. She also promotes a program called "Stop the Teasing" which is designed to help kids realize how badly teasing can hurt others.

Jon Scieszka and Lane Smith
http://www.chucklebait.com/

This interesting site provides biographical information about Scieszka and Smith. The "Fun Stuff" section offers a game for visitors to play and "Ask Beefsnakstik" a question. Visitors to the site can send an e-mail message and be on a mailing list.

Dr. Seuss
http://www.randomhouse.com/seussville/

Children will love the games and contests found at this excellent Random House Web site that focuses on books by Dr. Seuss; not on the author. There are games, contests, a posting of Seuss events, a catalogue and more.

Audrey Wood and Dan Wood
http://www.audreywood.com/

This terrific site offers activities for children (coloring pages, activity pages). Areas within the site include "Meet the Artists: Audrey Wood and Don Wood," "Lost and Found," "Activities," "Awards," and "Contests." "The Fan Bag" offers membership information and an art show for fans. "Top Secret" reveals the illustrators' secrets behind their books, and a special area, "Teachers, Parents, and Librarians," gives information about books and where to find them as well as a schedule of school visits, e-mail, newsletter, and an educational clubhouse.

CONCLUSION

The World Wide Web offers such a wealth of information that some educators cannot imagine developing a program without it. For many media specialists, great Web sites inspire their finest programs. In this age of technology, the Internet is an invaluable resource thanks to accurate, reputable sites that enhance program planning and provide solid program support.

Chapter 7

Extending, Evaluating, and Assessing Library Media Programs

Although library media specialists must remain focused on the present throughout the entire process of planning and executing a program, evaluating the program also requires looking to both the past and the future. After the program itself is completed, the media specialist must assess what worked and what did not, what is worth repeating, and what needs revising for more efficient and effective programming the next time.

Sue Wiley knew not to be lulled into a feeling of closure on her program even though the rewards were many.

I knew my program was a hit even before words of praise came my way. As I stood at the back of the library media center watching the guest speaker, I could feel the children's energy soar. They paid attention, laughed at the right times, and asked questions that told me they were learning the objectives I set.

Following the program, teachers and students thanked me throughout the day. Even the principal sang my praises during announcements the next morning. After all my hard work paid off, I was so tempted to merely drop all the program material in a box, stash it away till next year, and pat myself on the back for a job well done.

But I knew I wanted to make sure students actually learned, and to ensure that similar programs in the future would be effective. That required evaluation.

After the day of her program events, Sue knew that her work was still not complete. For students, she needed to extend the learning through follow-up activities. For participants, acknowledgments must be sent thanking them for their contributions. For the media specialist, formal evaluations were needed to assess the program's merits and weaknesses.

These stages following the actual event may seem anticlimactic, but they are relevant and necessary for students, guests and volunteers, and especially the media specialist, who will want to make the next program easier and more effective.

EXTENDING THE PROGRAM

Activities for Students in the School Library Media Center

During the planning stage, the library media specialist should consider the activities for the school library media center that will follow the program. Depending on the complexity of the program, these activities may require various amounts of time. For example, one program featured a display entitled "Eating Utensils from Around the World." In the follow-up activity for this display, the media specialist involved third-graders in a lively discussion on the topic and an overview of the related books found in the school library media center.

Some media specialists use learning centers as a means of extending a program. For example, following the "Eating Utensils" display, the media specialist created a learning center related to the topic. The center focused on "Table Setting." Youngsters were invited to visit the center, which included a small round table covered with an attractive linen cloth. China, crystal, silverware, napkins, and table decorations were available. A cookbook that illustrates how to set a table was displayed at the center. They were then encouraged to set the table and verify that they did it correctly by looking at the cookbook and a poster illustrating the proper table setting.

Other centers in the school library media facility may focus on research into the program topic. Following the "Eating Utensils" display, a media specialist could use that theme to research the utensils that people from various countries use when eating. At the research center, the media specialist could provide a worksheet that lists different countries to research and books that focus on the topic.

Following a program, book displays and bulletin board displays can also be used as extended activities in the library media center. Promoting books related to the program is a simple yet effective continuation of any event. Not surprisingly, media specialists typically find that book circulation increases tremendously for the program topic area, and books placed on display are often checked out immediately.

Activities for Students in the Classroom

Media specialists will want to encourage teachers to extend the knowledge or skills learned during the school library media program into the classroom. To do so, provide teachers with a bibliography of trade books, reference resources, and addresses of Web sites related to the subject. If there is a district professional library, media specialists can order the related professional materials to have on hand for teachers. They will also want to put all these materials on reserve for specific grade levels or classes to use. Some media specialists carry this a step further and give teachers recommended classroom activities to follow specific programs. Others invite specific classes or grade levels to the school library media center to participate in the learning centers that the media specialist created on the topic.

Extended classroom activities following a program are usually generated by classroom teachers. For example, one school library media program for fifth-graders featured three guest speakers who demonstrated fingerpainting, collage, and papier-mâché to small groups simultaneously. Following the program, teachers extended it by including a classroom art project in which students were asked to select from one of the three art media and create a product that focused on a specific class theme. Afterward, students were encouraged to display their creations in the school library media center.

Like extension work provided in the media center, follow-up activities for the classroom can also include learning centers related to a program theme. Program-related games, worksheets, art, and writing are common center activities that children enjoy.

WRAPPING IT UP

Thank-You to Resource People and Places

Immediately following the special event, show your appreciation to the resource people and/or companies that participated in the program. The power of gratitude cannot be overemphasized. More than any other interaction with program participants and volunteers, acknowledging their work and efforts will have a long-lasting and far-reaching effect.

Regardless of the ease or difficulty of the program, the speaker or business should receive an acknowledgment. This can be handled in several ways. For some guests you may feel that a less formal letter is appropriate. In that case, you may choose to send a handwritten note thanking the guest. For the speakers representing a company or business, it is important to send a formal thank-you, preferably typed and on school letterhead to the guest speaker. Also, ask speakers if they would like you to send a letter to the business they represented. Although it would seem appropriate to do so in all situations, occasionally library media specialists have found themselves in the uncomfortable situation of having sent a letter to the business, only to discover that the speaker had not secured permission to participate in the program on company time. Such cases may be rare, but they are worth noting here so that all acknowledgments fulfill their positive intent.

In many cases, principals are receptive to sending the thank-you letter to the program speaker themselves. A letter from the school principal on school letterhead is often cherished by presenters, and it can impressively highlight one's professional credits. Even if the principal agrees to send the formal acknowledgment, an additional note of appreciation from the media specialist is still in order.

Some library media specialists enjoy presenting certificates of appreciation in place of notes. Others invite the presenters and volunteer staff to a luncheon, breakfast, or similar event that recognizes them. Regardless of the way in which the program participants are acknowledged, anyone making a contribution to the program appreciates an expression of gratitude. Most of all, the library media specialist's thoughtfulness will be remembered for a long time, creating receptivity to future requests for participation in program activities.

Some of the best thank-yous come from the students themselves. Teachers are often eager for students to have real-life experiences with writing thank-you notes, and this presents an ideal opportunity for children to learn how to write a thank-you note. Many students include their own original art as a way of expressing appreciation. For particularly special programs that made a significant contribution to the school, some teachers videotape or audiotape the student thank-yous. Media specialists sometimes encourage this form of appreciation by discussing the possibilities with the classroom teachers and offering to deliver the material to the resource person.

Thank-You to Volunteers

Others who helped make the program possible should also be acknowledged through a handwritten note, typed letter, or certificate of appreciation. Thank-yous should be sent to teachers, volunteers, parents, ancillary staff, the PTA, and any other people who supported the program. All these persons deserve some sort of acknowledgment. Although honoring volunteers at the end of the school year with a special reception is an excellent way of expressing your appreciation, remember that an expression of gratitude from you immediately following the program is always meaningful and appropriate.

Updating the Community
Resources File

Chapter 5 provides details for establishing a community resources file. Even though volunteers will be updating the file at least once a year, it is essential to update it following the program as well. Add new and eliminate outdated information. The following considerations will assist in updating the community resources file after the program:

- Record a brief explanation of how you used the resources for the program.

- Correct, add, or delete information such as fees, contact persons, and supplemental resources.

- Include information on any new features incorporated into the program.

- Write a brief summary of positive and negative responses from students and teachers.

- Add new resources to the file.

- Delete files if necessary.

It is particularly important to make notations concerning the community resource people. Beyond noting their general effectiveness as presenters, make certain to note whether their ideas and vocabulary were at the right level for the students. Assessing the topic is equally important. Consider questions such as: Did it pique students' interest as much as you had hoped? Was the material appropriate for the audience? Did it provide relevant and dynamic support for the students' curriculum? Answers to such questions should be recorded in the community resources file and reviewed before the program is presented again.

EVALUATING THE PROGRAM

Informal Evaluations

Just as Sue Wiley evaluated her program by observing student responses to the guest speaker, many library media specialists begin assessing their program in progress. Afterward, they draw additional conclusions by reflecting on all stages of the program. At either time, informal evaluations are sturdy springboards to the overall assessment of a program.

By the Library Media Specialist

Before formally evaluating the program, sit down after the event and reflect on how well you think it went. Did it meet your original goals? How did the audience react? Did the program hold your interest? What were its strengths? What would you do differently if you had the opportunity? Trust your instincts. Even before asking, you often know deep down how the program really went.

By the Faculty and Students

Consider the essential feedback from faculty and students. Their nonverbal cues during the presentation say a great deal. Looks of interest or boredom on their faces during the program are as revealing as their comments. Opinions expressed during conversations, whether enthusiastic or critical, provide clues concerning the success of the program. They are also worth considering when developing the next program topic. (Some media specialists record comments in a journal for future use.)

An obvious goal of programming is to interest students in checking out and reading books. Therefore, observation of student and faculty visits to the media center can offer some insight into the success of the program. When students and teachers are really excited about a topic, there is usually an increase in the circulation of books and use of the school library media center. Media specialists, therefore, hope to see the circulation of books soar, particularly in the category related to the program topic. Children's interest in browsing book displays and participating in learning centers related to the program is an additional indicator of a successful program. Another indirect sign of a program's success is increased circulation of books on related topics.

Teachers' involvement in extended activities following the program also illustrates the success of the program. Not surprisingly, enthusiastic responses to an effective program translate into long-term interest in the topic well after the event has ended. If your program topic is extended into the classroom through a specific teacher-generated lesson or activity, you know your work inspired that teacher.

Library media specialists absorb a great deal by observing changes in teachers and students following the program. They look for, and ideally hope to discover, schoolwide enthusiasm for the topic. Seeing teachers use the program as a springboard for activities in the classroom is a sure sign of program success. Noticing a change in attitude about the library media center by formerly uninterested students is another sign. Naturally, seeing students excited about the topic or skill related to the library program, responding to requests for more books on the topic, and helping students find more related resources in the reference section are all strong indicators of the program's impact.

Formal Evaluations

By the Library Media Specialist

Library media specialists will want to use the form in Figure 7.1, which is based on the original program planning checklist, to evaluate the success of the program. This form allows for considering items such as the facility and support resources as well as the individual speaker when assessing the total program. After completing this formal evaluation, media specialists can then analyze the data.

MEDIA SPECIALIST PROGRAM EVALUATION

Using the five-point Likert scale below, please circle the response that best describes how effectively the program item was met.

	INEFFECTIVE				EFFECTIVE
PROGRAM CHECKLIST	1	2	3	4	5
Interest for theme	1	2	3	4	5
Accomplished goals	1	2	3	4	5
Resources selected	1	2	3	4	5
Materials selected	1	2	3	4	5
Publicity	1	2	3	4	5
Scheduling process	1	2	3	4	5
Volunteers	1	2	3	4	5
Furniture and room arrangement	1	2	3	4	5
Seating arrangement	1	2	3	4	5
Traffic flow	1	2	3	4	5
Preparation of AV equipment	1	2	3	4	5
Lighting	1	2	3	4	5
Decorations, displays, exhibits	1	2	3	4	5
Guest speaker	1	2	3	4	5
OVERALL PROGRAM	**1**	**2**	**3**	**4**	**5**

Figure 7.1. Media specialist program evaluation form.

By the Teachers

Formal evaluations by teachers and students are invaluable assessment tools. While the program is still fresh in their memories, provide them with simple forms like the one in Figure 7.2, listing clearly stated questions about the program. When developing the evaluation form, consider the following points:

- Seek feedback immediately following the program.
- Design a simple instrument with ease of completion in mind.
- Design an instrument with ease of tabulation in mind.
- Structure your questions carefully so as to obtain the true reaction of the person.
- Provide for open-ended comments.
- Assure anonymity for the person completing the form.
- Collect the responses in a timely manner.

It is important to find out how teachers think the program related to the curriculum and personal needs of students. That feedback alone can determine whether a similar program is in order for the future. Additionally, teacher responses also suggest other program needs.

By the Students

To get the best input, have students fill out an evaluation form as soon after the program as possible. Library media specialists may design their own forms or use one of the sample forms in Figure 7.3, page 130, and Figure 7.4, page 131.

(Text continues on page 132.)

OPINION NEEDED

Faculty Program Evaluation

Program Topic: _____

Date of Program: _____

Using the five-point Likert scale below, please circle the response to each statement that best describes the effectiveness of the school library media program.

	INEFFECTIVE				EFFECTIVE
ITEM					
Program topic met student interests.	1	2	3	4	5
Program enriched the curriculum.	1	2	3	4	5
Program provided new information.	1	2	3	4	5
Speaker spoke at the right level.	1	2	3	4	5
Speaker held audience's attention.	1	2	3	4	5
OVERALL PROGRAM	**1**	**2**	**3**	**4**	**5**

Would you recommend that we invite this speaker back next year? Why or why not?

_____

_____

_____

What other topics would you suggest for a school library media program?

_____

_____

_____

List the strengths of the program.

_____

_____

_____

Describe the weaknesses of the program.

_____

_____

_____

Figure 7.2. Faculty program evaluation form.

LIBRARY PROGRAM

Circle the face that shows how you feel.

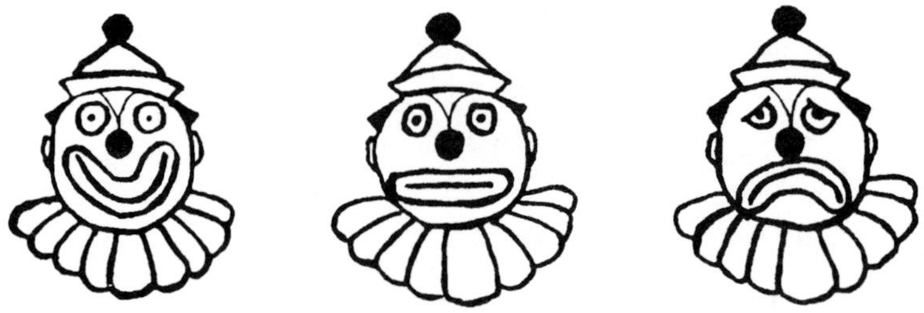

1. I liked the program.

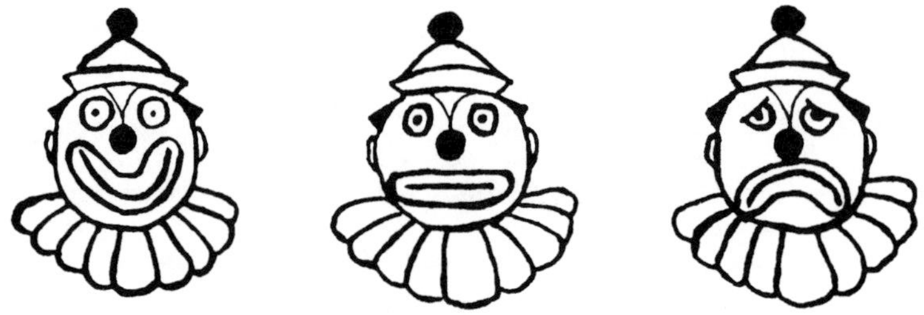

2. I hope we have another library program.

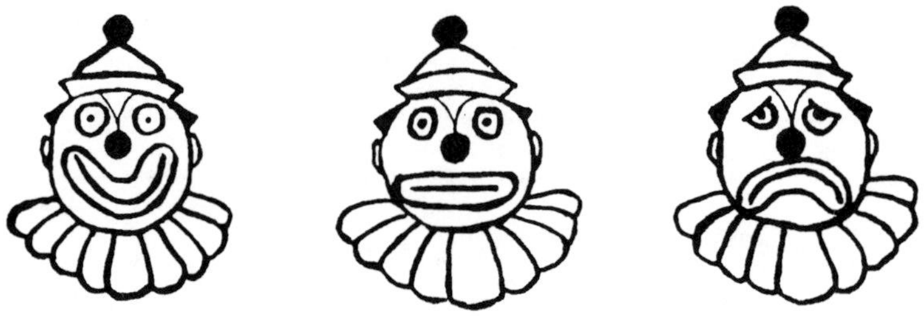

3. I want to take a library book home this week.

Figure 7.3. Sample program evaluation for primary students.

WANTED!

YOUR OPINION ABOUT THE GUEST SPEAKER

I enjoyed hearing the speaker.   Yes _____ No _____

I could hear the speaker well.   Yes _____ No _____

I could easily see the speaker and the material he or she showed.   Yes _____ No _____

I want to find out more information about this topic.   Yes _____ No _____

I read at least one book on the topic before the program.   Yes _____ No _____

I want to read a book about the topic soon.   Yes _____ No _____

I would like to attend another special program in the school
        library media center.   Yes _____ No _____

The part of the program I enjoyed most was:

_____

_____

_____

The part of the program I liked least was:

_____

_____

_____

I would like the school library media center to sponsor a program about:

_____

_____

_____

_____

**PLEASE RETURN THIS FORM TO YOUR TEACHER, WHO WILL PUT
IT IN THE SUGGESTION BOX IN THE SCHOOL LIBRARY MEDIA
CENTER.**

Figure 7.4. Sample program evaluation for students, grades 4–6.

Circulation Data and Usage

To determine the success of a particular program, examine circulation of books and materials by students and teachers following a special program. A goal of most programs is to increase the circulation of books as well as the library usage. The data should provide you with the number of books circulated, types of books circulated, and the student populations that checked them out. A significant increase in circulation immediately following a program usually confirms its success.

Examining the number of classes (and grade levels) that visit the school library media center also gives some indication of program success. Circulation data as a program evaluation tool will offer clues as to whether future programs on the topic will garner enthusiastic responses.

ASSESSING THE PROGRAM

Examine and Analyze the Data

After collecting and recording the data, examine and analyze them. Keep in mind that all data are not quantifiable. You must take into consideration the qualitative data as well. Look at the reported strengths and weaknesses of the program gleaned from the comments. Your goal using this information is to answer two questions: Should I consider offering this program again? If yes, what can be done to make it better next time?

Informal Data

Consider the informal data that you gathered. Comments, enthusiastic responses, and general usage of the library media center are all factors that cannot be easily measured but can be used to refine future programs.

Formal Data

Evaluation Forms Data. As soon as students and teachers return their completed evaluations, analyze the data and then use the results to plan future programs. The input should provide a solid overview of the program's strengths and weaknesses. It should also determine once and for all if you met your goals. Keep in mind that even after the best of programs, library media specialists still compile a list of ways to improve or strengthen future programs on the same topic. Among the data, you will find many suggestions for other program topics that interest students and teachers.

The evaluations will also give you some idea of how to better plan for traffic flow, seating, and general logistical elements that are best determined by trial and error. Most important, use all feedback as an invitation to sharpen your skills and spur further creativity. Do not take constructive suggestions as insults. See them all as helpful tips that will improve future programs.

Circulation Data. A major goal for most programs includes an increase in circulation. In fact, media specialists occasionally target specific low-circulating areas and develop an interesting program that focuses on that area, with the major intent of increasing book circulation. Following all programs, examine the circulation data for the next several months. Compare data gathered following the program to circulation data gathered during the previous weeks and months. Programming can effect an increase in circulation in general or an increase in the circulation of certain parts of the library's collection. Note whether the books in the program category and related categories are being checked out more frequently by students and faculty. Consider the number of materials circulated, the type of user (grade level, student, faculty), and types of materials (books, magazines, media) as well as the subject area of the material. These are often important indicators of a successful special event.

Record the Results

The question is: What do you do with the results once you have them? Begin making use of them immediately. Determine whether to invite the speaker back and record the decision on that person's community resources card. If the speaker is to come back, add your own comments about that person, as well as any relevant feedback from teachers and students. Include notes about how to improve the program. After collecting valuable information through assessment forms, personal notes, and statistical data, be sure to make the most of it.

CREATING REPORTS AND RECORDS

Develop a Program Report

Pulling together both the formal and informal data collected during and after the program is essential. Ultimately, this information will go into a report that focuses on the strengths and weaknesses of the program as well as the extended influences of the program that continue long after it is completed.

Besides being a dynamic tool for you, the report will also prove helpful to the school at large. Share portions of the report with your principal, who, if an effective administrator, will be interested in the data. Information gathered, such as increased circulation following the program (see Figure 7.5) and requests by teachers for specific books to be ordered, will be strong indicators of your facility's strengths and needs. Your principal will likely include some of your data in reports to the district. Often this type of information can be used to support budget requests for the library media center or to write grant proposals to fund the school library collection. As anyone who has written grant proposals knows, most grant requests are fulfilled because of need, not merely desire. What better way to demonstrate need than by including specific information such as that accumulated before and after a special program on a topic?

Sharing this information with the principal also offers more personal benefits. Often, the self-assessment of your work will add markedly to your yearly evaluation, because your data are concrete indicators that you have a strong grasp not only on creating effective programs but also on determining their success.

PROGRAM DESCRIPTIVE STATISTICS

Number of publicity notices appearing through local media   _____

Number of classes invited to participate   _____

Number of classes actually participating   _____

Number of students participating in the program   _____

Number of requests for additional information on topic   _____

Average weekly circulation of entire school prior to program
    (for eight weeks)   _____

Average weekly circulation of entire school following the program
    (for eight weeks)   _____

Miscellaneous notes:

_____

_____

_____

_____

_____

_____

Figure 7.5. Sample form for program descriptive statistics.

Your report should include your original program plan, sample evaluation forms, and charts and graphs that display the results. With all this information plainly laid out for the principal and school district administrators, they are made aware of all the demands and rewards of programming.

CONCLUSION

More than any other single activity that a media specialist can engage in, a program offers the most far-reaching and powerful results. The effects of a successful school library program resonate throughout the school for an extended period of time. Books on the program topic continue to be checked out; teachers extend the topic into their classrooms; and students search the Internet in their quest for more information on the topic. Occasionally, programs have lifelong impacts, as in the case of one youngster who decided to become a writer and began writing stories following a presentation by a local author.

In many cases, a strong program also inspires teachers with fresh ideas. Additionally, seeing outstanding work beyond the realm of usual duties sparks new respect from administrators. Often, the entire climate of a school can shift thanks to an extraordinary event.

The benefits move beyond the school, too. Programs draw together members of the community. Parents interact with business representatives. Contributing resources from business and industry add richly to the overall impact made on children. Volunteers from outside the school may view the faculty, school, and even education in a better light. Publicity generated by programs enhances the reputation of the school. Even groups who do not participate in the event hear about its impact from students, friends, and co-workers.

Unquestionably, the impact of programming is dynamic and extensive. Although much credit will rightly be given to the teachers and volunteers, without whom the program could not occur, the real honors will go to you. Personally and professionally, the rewards you will reap from successful programming will always exceed your greatest expectations.

Chapter **8**

Dynamic Model Programs and Ideas That Really Work

Even media specialists most excited about programming shared with us concerns about finding the time and creative energy to develop programs. To address this issue, we surveyed library media specialists across the United States and gathered clear, well-developed program ideas that have already proven successful. Many contributing media specialists received the School Librarian of the Year Award from their state organization. Others are former presidents of their state school library association. All have received high recommendations from their state or district school library directors.

Every contributing media specialist is recognized for exceptional programming. In addition to listing these outstanding professionals and their credentials in this chapter, their names appear with each program idea they contributed. When no credit line appears, the program tip is a culmination of ideas submitted by three or more media specialists.

Feedback from the survey (see Appendix A) mailed to the library media specialists indicated both consistent patterns and inspiring ingenuity. Not surprisingly, the three most common forms of programming are book fairs, storytelling, and author visits. Yet even in familiar contexts, these exemplary programs stand out, especially in originality and community support in the form of speakers, volunteers, and resources.

This chapter highlights more than 100 model programs and ideas. Some are original programs described in depth, others offer clever twists to familiar ideas. Feel free to use the program suggestions exactly as they appear, or modify them to fit your particular needs. You may even want to design your own program by combining different ideas. In any case, let each contribution inspire you to develop your own programs.

The model programs and ideas are divided into four sections:

1. Programs for Everyone

2. Programs for Students
    Curriculum: Reading/Language Arts
    Curriculum: Beyond Reading/Language Arts
    Personal Interests
    Holidays and Special Events

3. Programs for Teachers

4. Programs for Parents

CONTRIBUTORS OF
MODEL PROGRAMS AND IDEAS

Suzanne Baxley
Brooklyn Springs Elementary School
Lancaster, South Carolina
Lancaster County Schools
South Carolina Association of School
    Librarians, Media Specialist of
    the Year, 1998
Lancaster County Library Media
    Specialist Association, Chair,
    1992-1994

Vicki Carter Broussard
Lake Arthur Elementary School
Lake Arthur, Louisiana
Jefferson Davis Parish Schools

Karen Czerwinski
Lulu M. Ross Elementary School
Milford, Delaware
Milford School District
Delaware's School Library Media
    Association, Outstanding School
    Library Media Specialist Award,
    1998

Julie Godfrey
Memorial Drive Elementary School
Houston, Texas
Spring Branch Independent School
    District
Crystal Apple Award for Excellence
    in Education, Spring Branch
    Independent School District,
    1998

Julie Hardegree
Edward White Elementary School
El Lago, Texas
Clear Creek Independent School
    District

Penny Hayne
Lake Murray Elementary School
Chapin, South Carolina
School District Five of Lexington
    and Richland Counties
South Carolina Association of School
    Librarians, President, 1999-2000

Pam Kanoy
Pilot Elementary School
Thomasville, NC
Guilford County Schools
North Carolina Association of School
    Librarians, Carolyn Palmer
    Media Coordinator of the Year,
    1996

Bonnie Keith
Bales Intermediate School
Friendswood, Texas
Friendswood Independent School
    District

Susan Link
Colony Bend Elementary School
Sugar Land, Texas
Fort Bend Independent School
    District
John Newbery Award Committee,
    Association of Library Services
    to Children, 2000
Mildred Batchelder Award
    Committee, American Library
    Association, 1999

Mary Lough
Margaret Beeks Elementary School
Blacksburg, Virginia
Montgomery County Public Schools
Virginia Education Media
    Association, School Library
    Media Specialist of the Year, 1998
Virginia Education Media
    Association, Roanoke Regional
    Director, 1990-1992

Phyllis Mays
Code Elementary School
Seneca, South Carolina
School District of Oconee
South Carolina Association of School
    Librarians, Media Specialist of
    the Year, 1997
Seneca Lions Club Educator of the
    Year, 1997-1998
Teacher of the Year, Code
    Elementary, 1989-1990

Marilyn Mitchell
Mae Smythe Elementary School
Pasadena, Texas
Pasadena Independent School District

Joan Moore
Lyndon Johnson Elementary School
Bryan, Texas
Bryan Independent School District
Reading Renaissance Model Library,
    1998-1999
Professional Specialist of the Year,
    Johnson Elementary, 1997-1999

Betty Anne Smith
Royall Elementary School
Florence, South Carolina
Florence School District One
South Carolina Association of School
    Librarians, Media Specialist of
    the Year, 1990
South Carolina Association of School
    Librarians, President, 1997-98
Florence School District One, Teacher
    of the Year, 1995 and 1996
Teacher of the Year, Royall
    Elementary, 1991

Jay Stailey
Bales Intermediate School
Friendswood, Texas
Friendswood Independent School
    District
Principal, former library media
    specialist, celebrity storyteller

Debby Stone
Fair-Oak Elementary School
Westminster, South Carolina
School District of Oconee
South Carolina Association of School
    Librarians, President, 1989

Donna Sullivan-Macdonald
Orchard School
South Burlington, Vermont
South Burlington School District

Marti Turner
River Oaks Baptist School
Houston, Texas
Private School

Sarah Wahl
Goose Creek Consolidated
    Independent School District
Baytown, Texas
Head Librarian of District

Patty Williams
George Washington Elementary
    School
Kingsport, Tennessee
Kingsport City Schools
Tennessee Association of School
    Librarians, Past President
Progressive School Library Media
    Award
Kingsport City School System
    Teacher of the Year, 1999

PROGRAMS FOR EVERYONE

To promote reading, the three model programs below garnered support from families, students, teachers, and community members. All three programs incorporate a clever twist for increasing the book collection. We have included this special events section because they encompass every area of the curriculum, and cover topics of interest to students, teachers, and parents. Each of the programs highlighted below includes a book fair which is the most common form of programming.

Book Fair Extravaganza

Julie Godfrey, Memorial Drive Elementary School, Houston, Texas, Spring Branch Independent School District

Julie's book fair (see Photo 8.1) is so grand an extravaganza that she prepares for it year round. Because she believes that tailoring the book selection to the audience is central to the event's success, she generates a continual book "wish list" as she reads review journals and publishers' catalogs, and while she attends conferences and shops at bookstores. Additionally, she encourages teachers and students to contribute to the list, which she ultimately submits to her book fair company four months before her November event.

Photo 8.1. Students enjoy browsing the annual book fair extravaganza. (*Memorial Drive Elementary School, Houston, Texas, Spring Branch Independent School District*)

Julie publicizes the fair generously within the school and throughout the community. According to Julie, signs and flyers—both within and beyond the school—are the most effective of all promotional efforts. Media center volunteers create and distribute newsletters to administrators and community leaders. Invitations to the book fair include a calendar of special events as well as a book order form for those who would like to purchase books for themselves or purchase and donate books to the media center. She also sends a calendar of events to parents along with a request for volunteers to work during the fair. Julie emphasizes that the fair would not be possible without the support of these generous volunteers.

To further market the event, she organizes special programs for students, parents, and teachers, the pinnacle of which is bringing guest authors to campus to speak and to autograph books. For example, each year she has a "Ladies Special Lunch." One year the event's guest was the author of a cookbook, who shared lunch with the mothers and other guests. At the book fair the author offered warm snacks prepared from her recipes and signed books beside a special display of "Hot New Books Not to Be Missed." Other events include a "Dad's Special Night." Even when the special event targets a specific group, Julie opens the affair to the community at large and invites everyone: parents, children, teachers, and community members.

In addition to the usual array of tables filled with books, a donation table dubbed "Friends of the Library" is prominently displayed. As parents and other Friends purchase books for the library in honor of whomever they wish, Julie attaches a special permanent book plate containing the name of the honoree inside the book. She then makes certain that the student honorees are the first to check out their special books. Because of Julie's ambitious advertising efforts, her unique and extensive book selection, and the memorable touches from her special event, her book fair enjoys a clientele of parents and community leaders who continue to attend even after the students have left the school.

Julie's keys to good book fairs:

- Develop a theme for the book fair.

- Use a good book fair company.

- Provide extensive input into the selection of books for the fair.

- Include a generous selection of books.

- Advertise extensively.

- Incorporate special touches that attract parents, student, and community members.

- Encourage parents to volunteer to help.

- Spend time organizing volunteers.

- Encourage teacher support by asking them for input on the "wish list" and using a portion of the book fair proceeds to purchase professional resources for faculty.

Reading Festival

Marti Turner, River Oaks Baptist School, Houston, Texas

The focus of the annual Reading Festival at River Oaks Baptist School is to promote reading. However, the annual event also raises money for the book collection. Marti does not actually sell books to individuals during a reading festival. Instead, she works toward raising money for book purchases.

In the spring, Marti uses her regular book budget to pre-order the books for her fall festival. Then she invites a wide range of guests to focus on a variety of content areas to pique reader interest. In the past, guest readers have included local politicians, police officers, university and school coaches, pediatricians, ballet stars, and a docent from the zoo who brought animals with her. But Marti goes even further by inviting stars beyond her community. Some years her celebrity readers have included a mascot for a sports team, disc jockeys, and musical groups, as well as nationally known author Louis Sachar, and storyteller Tom McDermott.

When the books arrive, Marti processes them and displays them at the Reading Festival, where Friends of the Library listen to readings then browse with the intent to purchase the books as a donation to the media center collection. When someone purchases a book (at list price), Marti places a bookplate inside that honors whomever the purchaser desires. After the event, she sends a thank-you note to the donor, and an acknowledgment to the honoree.

Her festival is a huge success with the parent, student, teacher, and community participants. Last year over 1,000 books were donated, at an estimated value of over $18,000.

Marti credits the success of her program to the school administration, faculty, and generous parents; careful planning; and most of all to wonderful volunteers.

Family Reading Night

Joan Moore, Johnson Elementary School, Bryan, Texas, Bryan Independent School District

Joan hosts Family Reading Night (see Photo 8.2, page 144) in conjunction with the Fall Book Fair each year during Children's Book Week in November at this U.S. Department of Education National Blue Ribbon School. She opens the event to the entire student body (about 350) and their families. For one night, families listen to celebrity readings and then attend the book fair.

Throughout the year, Joan keeps a file of potential "celebrities" to invite. To prepare for the actual event, she invites various community and state leaders, local television personalities, authors, storytellers, university athletes, and student body representatives to participate. In addition to their specific reading preference, Joan also inquires about their accomplishments and interests. This added information is invaluable, as she selects reading material for those celebrities who do not specify a particular work. She also uses it to write brief introductions for her teachers or parent volunteers to make before the celebrity reads or presents. Joan strives for a variety of speakers and readers so there will be something that appeals to everyone. She usually has 14 to 16 readers, including one or two reading in Spanish. About five days prior to the event, she sends reminder letters to all readers with directions to the school and other information.

Photo 8.2 A guest expert on Beatrix Potter is one of the many "celebrities" sharing stories and information with parents and students at Joan Moore's "Family Reading Night." *(Johnson Elementary School, Bryan, Texas, Bryan Independent School District)*

Ten days before the event, she sends home a sign-up sheet listing all the celebrities and their special presentation plans. Each family picks its top four choices. As forms are returned to her, Joan numbers them in the order they are received and then fills the sessions on a first reply, first served basis. She finds it best to keep each group at around 30 people.

Every family is assigned to two sessions, each 20 to 25 minutes long. She records their program choices on an assignment sheet available for pick up on arrival at Family Reading Night. Although assigning the guests to sessions takes considerable time, it ensures balanced attendance at all sessions and avoids the embarrassment of poorly attended sessions. In this way, every reader enjoys a good audience. (Clearly, says Joan, scheduling and organizing this event are the most difficult and time-consuming tasks. The event itself is great.)

To publicize Family Reading Night, in addition to sending letters (in English and Spanish) home to parents describing the events and asking them to sign up, Joan also generates excitement among students. Her student helpers perform skits about the event on the school's live, televised morning announcements. Other students make posters and decorate bulletin boards promoting the big night. She also publicizes the event on local television, on the radio, and in the local English- and Spanish-language newspapers.

Joan recruits teachers to greet and introduce each reader at the event. She always has two to three people in the front hallway at a table to sign up late registrants. Four people pass out assignment sheets. Additionally, she posts maps of the building along the hallways to help guests locate the readers' rooms.

To begin the night, the principal rings chimes and welcomes everyone over the intercom. The chimes ring again to end the first session and to begin the second. At the end of the second session Joan invites everyone to visit the Book Fair in the cafeteria. At the Book Fair, someone dressed in a story character costume (such as Clifford) greets guests. (*Tip:* Ask your book fair company if they have book character costumes available to advertise the event.) Finally, Joan also has local authors autographing their books, which of course are on sale.

After the event, she sends a handwritten thank-you note to each reader. She also selects a new book to place in the library in honor of each reader.

This event runs smoothly thanks to a great deal of preplanning. Each year, Joan receives much positive feedback from children, parents, and colleagues. Attendance has grown over the years. At a school with only approximately 350 students, Family Reading Night generates between 300 and 350 participants. As both Joan and her principal agree, "It is always one of the highlights of the year." Many parents and children tell Joan that it is their favorite event, and many of the readers ask to return the next year because they have so much fun.

Examples of Joan's Guests and Their Contributions to Family Reading Night:

- Aggie Wranglers, Texas A & M University's dance group, read *Barn Dance* and danced.

- The Brazos Valley Troupe (12-18-year-old actors) performed some of their favorite "fractured" fairy tales.

- A former NFL official read a story about a football player.

- A Beatrix Potter expert told a story and shared items from her Beatrix Potter collection.

- A Texas A & M University math professor's class presented *Math Curse.*

- Two Aggie baseball players read the stories, *Apple Batter* and *My Lucky Hat.*

- The high school principal read *The Principal's New Clothes.*

- A local meteorologist shared *Cloudy with a Chance of Meatballs.*

◆ A family dramatized a story, *The Three Little Wolves and the Big Bad Pig.*

PROGRAMS FOR STUDENTS

Library programs for students extend far beyond reading and the language arts to support all curriculum areas. A learning objective in any discipline can inspire an entire program. Because they teach different concepts, subjects require varied approaches. For example, a social studies program on Native Americans would be vastly different from a math program on weights and measures.

But your creative opportunities do not stop there. Programs for students also include holidays and any topic of interest to young patrons. Clearly, your options are endless.

Curriculum: Reading/Language Arts

Storytelling

⚔ *Jay Stailey, principal, celebrity storyteller, former library media specialist, Bales Intermediate School, Friendswood, Texas, Friendswood Independent School District*

"Tips for Storytellers"

As a former library media specialist and a university instructor of storytelling, Jay recognizes the importance of this art. A noted storyteller who frequently performs at schools and is constantly asked to entertain students at the school where he is principal, Jay offers the following advice about storytelling: Library media specialists should develop an ongoing storytelling program in their media centers. Such a program can be done on a weekly or monthly basis, but as in the case of reading aloud to students, it should be established on a consistent basis. Such a program permits students to learn about the oral tradition of true folklore and to realize that these stories were handed down orally from generation to generation long before they were recorded.

There is great value in listening to stories that are not necessarily connected to books. We are in such a visual media in this day and age that we are constantly sharing pictures with stories. Seldom do we give students the opportunity to exercise their imaginations, creating their own mental images. Youngsters need this valuable opportunity. Although many storytellers share tales that have been published as books, media specialists should select and encourage storytellers who relate stories never published. We must let children see that there are also stories outside the written form.

Storytelling provides an excellent opportunity to include people from other cultures and to focus on their traditions. A good storyteller inspires people to tell stories. It is important that teachers as well as students learn more about storytelling. Therefore, the storytelling program that is begun in the media center should be continued in the classroom. Encourage students to perform storytelling in the classroom.

Following are tips provided by library media specialists from across the nation who focus on storytelling in their media centers:

- Invite parents who are noted for their storytelling to the media center to share stories.

- Showcase a separate storytelling area in the library media center. (*Note*: Some media specialists combine this area with the read-aloud area or author chair area.)

- See if you have an adult library volunteer who is a storyteller. Ask him or her to tell stories occasionally to the children in the library during their weekly class visit.

- Develop an ongoing grandparent storytelling program.

- Ask the public library for the names of storytellers who share tales from other cultures.

- Contact the local or state storytelling organization for recommended storytellers who may be available to schools (check the Internet for resources).

- Offer students a special program on "The Art of Storytelling" during which the storyteller discusses tips for telling good stories.

- Encourage classroom teachers to learn this art and to teach students to tell stories. (One elementary media specialist sponsors a storytelling contest for students. The winners of the contest are asked to share their stories in the library.)

❊ *Phyllis Mays, Code Elementary School, Seneca, South Carolina, School District of Oconee*

"Courtyard Storytellers"

Third-grade students are taught a storytelling unit by their teacher and library media specialist. After much practice, the students perform their stories for the school and community. Often, the storytellers are invited to perform at other events in the community.

"Young Storytellers Share with Primary Students"

Fifth-grade students are exposed to numerous guest storytellers and learn storytelling from their teacher. Students select stories to tell from various resources, and after much practice they share the stories with third-grade students in the school.

Author-Related Activities

Events and activities related to authors are frequently presented at the elementary level. Consider the possibilities discussed in the following subsections for introducing certain authors or books to students.

Author Visits. Media specialists who contributed programs for this book mentioned frequently that they invite authors to their school library media centers. Not surprisingly, famous authors may charge a considerable amount for a visit. In some districts, multiple schools combine resources to bring an author to their students. Occasionally, schools share authors with bookstores to make the visit more affordable. Sometimes media specialists choose to invite local authors and illustrators, who charge less while still delighting the student audiences. Media specialists who frequently include authors in their programs recommend ordering multiple copies of the author's books in advance so that students can read and prepare questions to ask on program day. See Appendix D for a bibliography of resources that can help you plan an author visit. Additionally, a selected list of Web sites for popular children's authors and illustrators is available in Chapter 6.

Julie Hardegree, Edward White Elementary School, El Lago, Texas, Clear Creek Independent School District

Julie recommends the Simon & Schuster Publishing Web site (www.simonsays.com/kids) as a first step to planning author visits. The site shares excellent tips for finding an author, planning the visit, ordering the books, and handling the day of the event.

Special Programs Highlighting Authors. In lieu of an author visit, focus on a special author for a month. One school library media center focused on Peggy Parish and her works. All of the author's stories were read aloud in the media center to the classes. Even the older students became involved as each grade level had a special activity related to the Amelia Bedelia series. For example, fourth-graders read the books and created puns. Fifth-graders developed their own Amelia Bedelia stories in groups. The best of the stories selected by each class were videotaped and shared with children in primary grades. All students researched Peggy Parish's life, using resources such as *Something About the Author* and *Major Authors and Illustrators* (see Appendix D). As a culminating event, a special "Amelia Bedelia Day" was held in the media center. Students were thrilled when a teacher, dressed like Amelia Bedelia, entered the library media center. Following the special event, learning centers and displays focused on Parish's life and works all month long.

�֎ *Julie Hardegree, Edward White Elementary School, El Lago, Texas, Clear Creek Independent School District*

Interest Center Highlighting a Specific Author. Authors do not always have to visit the school for students to become familiar with them. Julie Hardegree sets up author centers in the school library media center to highlight various children's authors. To attract attention she uses a catchy title such as "An Author a Day Keeps You Reading O.K.!" The center usually includes an attractive poster or sign that identifies the author, a photograph of the author (if available), biographical information on the author, and a display of his or her works. A fun activity such as a crossword puzzle focusing on the author is sometimes available. (*Note:* Appendix D and Chapter 6 provide lists of resources that can be used to locate information about authors and illustrators.)

Booktalks. Library media specialists can encourage students to become familiar with specific authors by preparing booktalks about their works. Before author visits, media specialists should consider presenting booktalks that highlight the author's works. Consult Appendix D for resources that provide valuable booktalk ideas.

Communication Skills

"Live News Program"

✖ *Patty Williams, George Washington Elementary School, Kingsport, Tennessee, Kingsport City School District*

Patty presents an unusual ongoing program sponsored by the school library media center. She broadcasts a live morning TV news program to every classroom. A team of five students, ages 8 to 10, are responsible for planning the mechanics of each daily broadcast for WSIC (Washington School Is Cool) (see Photo 8.3, page 150). Patty trains them to operate the digital video mixer, audio mixer, and two cameras. Other students serve as anchors, weather forecasters, reporters, and leaders of the Pledge of Allegiance. In addition to the daily announcements, typical segments feature activities in the classroom relating to curriculum, guest speakers, interviews with visiting authors, library promotion, and book reviews. Twice a week other students prepare and share jokes on the air. Also, a library research question relating to the current area of study is asked weekly and the winning student receives a free paperback book.

Photo 8.3. Media specialist Patty Williams directs students as they prepare to present the daily live broadcast from WSIC (Washington School Is Cool). *(George Washington Elementary School, Kingsport, Tennessee, Kingsport City Schools)*

Patty's goal is elaborate, but impressively clear. This empowers students to improve communication skills, give effective and organized verbal presentations, gain poise and self-confidence, promote teamwork, and celebrate their achievements. Students also learn to use new technology to creatively produce a morning program that relays information to the school population.

To select students, Patty solicits input from teachers about students with special talents and computer skills. The five students Patty chooses stay on duty for six weeks. During their final week, she brings on the next group so the students who are knowledgeable can train the new group. This results in a smooth transition.

When originally built, the school was wired for closed circuit television allowing Patty to use a professional broadcast system. Although many schools do not have such an elaborate system, modifications of this concept can be adapted, especially with advanced technology, computerized networking systems, and Channel 1 (or similar) systems now available in districts throughout the country.

Reading Aloud

✵ *Penny Hayne, Lake Murray Elementary School, Chapin, South Carolina, School District Five of Lexington & Richland Counties*

"Leader of the Pack"

Penny's "Leader of the Pack" is a terrific promotional program for reading. The success of the program is because of the collaborative efforts between Penny and her principal as well as Penny and the community. Once Penny selected the motorcycle theme, the assistant principal searched the available community resources. She found a "Harley Riding" parent of a student in the school who helped to connect them with other Harley riders. Penny and the assistant principal assembled the group of motorcycle enthusiasts. All were professionals—doctors, attorneys, engineers, teachers, etc.—who rode Harley Davidsons.

After finalizing plans for the "Harley Riders" with the help of her principal, Penny added a surprise element to her program that was sure to intrigue students. Then she met with classroom teachers at her school to explain the program and give them a schedule with an invitation for all class members.

The event took place on the teacher parking lot, where students stood for the first phase, then sat in the grass area nearby for the second. Divided into groups by grade level, the students were escorted by their teachers to the parking lot. Suddenly they heard a distant roar that grew louder as, to their shocked delight, a band of motorcycles zoomed onto the parking lot. As they stood in wide-eyed awe, students were thrilled when the passenger on the lead cycle, dressed in black leather pants, a fringed jacket, and boots, dismounted the bike and took off her helmet. It was the principal! (see Photo 8.4, page 152) The students went wild with excitement.

After the principal's introduction, students were separated into their respective groups and different motorcycle riders joined the various groups. Students explored the cycles at close range and were invited to ask questions. They learned that such bikes were extremely expensive; therefore, a person who is interested in such a machine would need to be able to read and be successful to purchase one.

The "Harley Riders" either sat on the ground with the students or sat on their bikes while they read to the students. Penny had carefully preselected the books on themes related to the read-aloud event and given them to the "Harley Riders" prior to the program so the readers could be better prepared.

Following the program, students who visited the library media center discovered new displays designed around the theme "Rev Up to Reading." Included were all the books the guests read to students in the parking lot.

Photo 8.4. School principal, Claire Thompson, leads the pack of read-aloud celebrities. *(Lake Murray Elementary School, Chapin, South Carolina, School District Five of Lexington and Richland Counties)*

Athough its major purpose was to promote the joy of reading, this program also offered a meaningful social lesson by helping to break stereotypes. By meeting and interacting with the program volunteers, students realized that most motorcycle enthusiasts do not fit the common negative image that is often depicted in many films. Instead, they met professional reading enthusiasts who enjoy, among many other hobbies, riding motorcycles.

Not surprisingly, this innovative event drew much publicity. The event invoked much discussion among the students and resulted in coverage in the local newspaper.

Additional ideas related to reading aloud are listed below:

- "Hats Off to Readers"—Students and faculty members wear hats of every description to greet guest readers from the community. *(Phyllis Mays, Code Elementary, Seneca, South Carolina, School District of Oconee)*

- "Readers in Uniform"—Readers from various occupations are invited to visit the school in appropriate uniforms. They read aloud to the students to show how important reading is in the work place. *(Phyllis Mays, Code Elementary, Seneca, South Carolina, School District of Oconee)*

- "Book the Chair"—In celebration of Grandparents' Day, grandparents come and read to the classes. *(Penny Hayne, Lake Murray Elementary, Chapin, South Carolina, District Five of Lexington and Richland Counties)*

Activities to Promote Reading

Sarah Wahl, Goose Creek Schools, Baytown, Texas, Goose Creek Consolidated Independent School District

"Traveling Trunks"

As head librarian for the district Sarah has developed and offers "ready-to-go programs" to the media specialists for check out. She has developed trunks that contain everything needed for special programming. Sarah recommends that media specialists develop such programs on a variety of topics and authors and share them throughout the district.

"Mother Goose." Media specialists enjoy checking out this program to share with K–2 children. The trunk provides the following items: a three-foot tall Mother Goose; a smaller stuffed Mother Goose for children to hold; a variety of Mother Goose books, including collections as well as individual poems; individual poems with poster pictures; lesson plans; posters for display in the school library media center; an audio cassette of Mother Goose rhymes; various props; Mother Goose nesting blocks with a rhyme, number, and alphabet letter on each block; and activities.

"Anne of Green Gables." Sarah enjoyed making this trunk about one of her favorite books, *Anne of Green Gables,* and its author. When she visited Prince Edward Island, Canada, the home of author Lucy M. Montgomery, Sarah picked up interesting items to include in the trunk. She began creating the trunk by writing a short biography about Lucy Montgomery and developing a display board on her life. These were placed in the trunk along with the following items: an Anne of Green Gables (20-inch doll); a collection of *Anne of Green Gables* books (abridged and unabridged versions); an interactive CD of the book; display boards with postcard scenes of Prince Edward Island depicting settings from the story; props and miniature items related to the story such as a tea set; and various activities.

Joan Moore, Johnson Elementary School, Bryan, Texas, Bryan Independent School District

"Theme Days"

Joan uses the following one-day activities, or theme days, to promote reading during National Library Week as well as at other times of the year. For each program, she sends home a letter telling parents about each event. During the school's live televised morning announcements, students perform skits to get everyone excited about the activities.

- "Cuddle up with a Good Book" by wearing sleep attire and bringing a favorite pillow or stuffed animal. (Some students were a little embarrassed at first, until they saw the coach in his nightshirt and stocking cap, and the library media specialist in her robe and Mickey Mouse house shoes.)
- "Sock It to Me" by wearing crazy socks on that Reading Day.
- "Dress as Your Favorite Story Character" (also have a parade throughout the building to show costumes).
- "See the World Through a Good Book" by wearing funny sunglasses.
- "Tie into a Good Book" and wear a funny tie.
- Take your "Hats Off to Readers" and wear an outrageous hat.

Local Programs

Phyllis Mays, Code Elementary, Seneca, South Carolina, School District of Oconee

Phyllis sponsors a variety of events to promote reading, among them:

- "Read & Succeed": A monthly advertisement to promote reading is displayed in the library media center. This special area is designed to encourage reading through themes with titles like "Under the Apple Tree," "In the Pumpkin Patch," and "Around Totem Pole." A photo bulletin board of readers is displayed in the hallway.
- "R and R" (Retire and Read): This program encourages senior citizens from a local retirement community to read to students.
- "FRAT Readers": *F*raternity *R*eaders *A*re *T*errific Readers is a philanthropic project for a service fraternity from Clemson University. Approximately 50 male college students visit every week to read to students. The purpose of the program is to have dependable and responsible males come to the school library media center to promote reading, thereby setting an example for the at-risk students who look to the volunteers as role models.
- "Books Funded by Kiwanis Club": The local Kiwanis Club funds books for the elementary schools throughout the city. In one year alone, a bumper sticker sale brought in almost $2,000 for purchasing new books.

State and National Programs

- "State-Level Book Award Programs": Many state school library organizations throughout the United States now sponsor a reading program in which a committee of media specialists and educators selects a list of (usually 15-25) books for elementary youngsters to read. Children choose the books from this list to read and must complete a specified number of books to vote for their favorite. The votes of children from across the state are tallied, and the winning book is added to the award list. Usually the author of the book is invited to the state school library organization conference to accept the award and deliver a speech at a luncheon. Check with your state organization to become involved in this special program. A packet of information detailing the program can be ordered along with incentives for participating students. (Names for the awards vary from state to state. For example, in Texas it is known as the Bluebonnet Award.)

- "Night of a Thousand Stars": A great program idea, originally sponsored by the American Library Association to celebrate National Library Week in April, is to host a "Night of a Thousand Stars" in your library media center. Invite as many celebrities as you can from your community (sports stars, news anchors, famous personalities, authors) to read a favorite bedtime story or poem or to share a special childhood memory about reading. Open the event to all interested participants throughout the community. Adults and children alike are thrilled to meet celebrities, especially in such a warm, noncompetitive atmosphere. If some of the celebrities are authors or illustrators, allow them to share their own work and to show the children how they, too, can begin a creative career like writing. Finally, keep in mind that the term *stars* is very broad. Principals, community members, special teachers, and even library media specialists can be stars.

- "Living Legends": This program, sponsored by the Library of Congress, is similar to "Night of a Thousand Stars." In this case, media specialists recognize local living legends by inviting them to a special event in the school library media center. They can discuss their careers and how the community has been affected by their work. Sports stars, local government officials, or anyone in the arts can be invited. However, also consider those less well-known but equally legendary people who have made outstanding contributions to their community. Contact American Library Association by calling 1-800-545-2433 or visit their

Web site at http://www.ala.org/ for more information on this program.

Bulletin Boards and Displays

- "Snap the Faculty." Take a photograph of each faculty member holding a favorite book. Using the ALA "Celebrity Read" posters as a model, photograph the individual holding one of his or her favorite books. Display these photographs in a display case or on a bulletin board in your school library media center. An alternative is to ask faculty members for personal photographs. Include their favorite book titles under the photographs. Although this idea promotes literature and reading with the students, it also provides an opportunity for students to get to know the teachers on campus. If your school has a Web site, consider using a digital camera to save the cost of film and processing.

- "Teachers' Favorites." Create a bulletin board with a paper tree. Take pictures of the teachers, mount them on red paper apples, and place them on the tree branches. Ask the teachers to tell you the title of a favorite children's book (or you may ask for a character). Next, mount these on paper apples and place them around the base of the tree. Challenge the students with a matching game to pair up the teacher apples with the title (or character) apples. Keep copies of the game sheets near the bulletin board. Award prizes to the winners. Prizes based on this theme could include apple notepads, apple supply boxes, an apple pencil, or apple stickers. Also display the teachers' favorite books.

  This idea can be modified to fit almost any theme. A particularly popular display includes separate photographs of the teachers and their pets for the students to match up. Include a display of pet books in the media center. A similar display could focus on teachers' favorite foods, and feature children's cookbooks.

Reading Incentive and Rewards Programs

Suzanne Baxley, Brooklyn Springs Elementary School, Lancaster, South Carolina, Lancaster County Schools

"Read-In." Suzanne and a colleague proposed and planned the first Read-In for their district. It has now become an annual program sponsored by the local library media specialists' association and includes all schools in Lancaster County, South Carolina. Each year, the sponsoring school chooses a place of special historical significance (for example, Andrew Jackson State Park or a historical building in downtown Lancaster) as the host site and encourages members of the community to tell stories, give historical talks, or share memories about the site. With enthusiastic help from the Historical Society, the event, rich with information about the people of Lancaster, draws impressive participation from adults and children alike. Often, time is included in the event for silent reading and a picnic lunch.

At the beginning of each school year, every school in the area determines its own criteria for selecting its ten students who can attend this one-day field trip. Naturally, emphasis is always placed on their commitment to reading.

⚔ *Bonnie Keith, Bales Elementary School, Friendswood, Texas, Friendswood Independent School District*

"Lock-In." A party is held near the end of the school year in the library to reward readers who have met specific reading goals (goals and criteria will vary from school to school). The Lock-In takes place from 6:30 p.m. to 11:00 p.m. on a Friday night, and activities include games such as bingo, a craft activity, free time in the gym, and storytelling in the library. Pizza and ice cream sundaes are served. Each student is asked to contribute $3.00. If students are unable to afford the fee, money is taken out of the media center budget. (The amount, times, and activities can vary. Some libraries sponsor a sleepover where students stay in the library media center all night. In the very best situations, the principal attends and performs storytelling or reads aloud to the students.)

⚔ *Suzanne Baxley, Brooklyn Springs Elementary School, Lancaster, South Carolina, Lancaster County Schools*

"Go for the Gold." Read 100 Books: Suzanne's reading incentive program targets the entire school. Early in the year, she sends letters to parents introducing the contest, and explains it in person to students at orientation and again to parents at the PTA Open House.

In the school foyer, Suzanne displays the contest objectives:

- ◆ Read 50 books = Bronze Medal Club
- ◆ Read 75 books = Silver Medal Club
- ◆ Read 100 books = Gold Medal Club

Additionally, all teachers create a reading success chart that they post in the classroom. Throughout the contest, students turn in a special form provided with their parents' signature each time they complete 10 books. For each incremental achievement, the student's teacher puts a sticker on the chart beside the student's name. Along the way, students receive prizes, awards, and recognition. Prizes for students who win the medals are determined by the library media specialist and the principal, whose budget money usually allows selection of more impressive prizes than the media specialist could afford alone.

Bonnie Keith, Bales Elementary School, Friendswood, Texas, Friendswood Independent School District

"Pizza with the Principal": After students read a set number of books, they are rewarded with a pizza party hosted by the principal. During the luncheon they sit and visit in the school library media center work room. This concept can be modified for continued use throughout the year. Students get to know their principal, staff, or media specialists during these luncheons. "Tea Time with the Counselor" and "Subs with the Assistant Principal" are other examples of fun-filled events that Bonnie promotes for her popular reading incentive programs.

Poetry

"Poetry Break"

"Poetry Break" is a time for students and teachers to experience a fun diversion and be exposed to poetry at the same time. Teachers voluntarily open their classrooms to a scheduled mini-session during which the library media specialist provides a poetry break. At the designated time, the media specialist visits the classroom and reads poetry to students for 15 minutes. Poetry topics related to current studies can be suggested by the teacher, or may be chosen by the media specialist to relate to an upcoming holiday or event.

The focus of the program is enjoyment. Wearing a costume, bringing a prop, or inviting a volunteer to enact a short skit that leads into the poem are all added surprises that pique students' interest. The media specialists who use this program regularly are firm believers that introducing children to poetry in a fun and entertaining context helps make poetry more accessible and interesting to them.

Julie Hardegree, Edward White Elementary School, El Lago, Texas, Clear Creek Independent School District

"P.I.G.—Poetry Is Great!"

Hold a poetry writing contest. Have students compose original poems to submit for a drawing. The poems are not judged, only randomly drawn (and read) for prizes. The poetry can be displayed in the school library media center.

Curriculum:
Beyond Reading/Language Arts

Commonly, media specialists extend their programming to include any number of subjects. Particularly favored by students and faculty alike are programs that highlight or incorporate multicultural studies and physical education. A list of other ideas for programs related to social studies, science, the arts, and other subject areas follows the three highlighted programs in this section.

Cultures and Countries of the World

✠ *Susan Link, Colony Bend Elementary School, Sugar Land, Texas, Fort Bend Independent School District*

"Book a Trip Around the World"

One schoolwide goal at Colony Bend Elementary is to raise awareness and understanding of cultures around the world. All the classroom teachers in the school focus on developing activities and learning experiences that meet this goal. The media specialist collaborates with the teachers to provide resources and activities that enrich the curriculum and support this goal. The year-long theme in the school library media center is "Book a Trip Around the Word." Susan says that commercial maps and bookmarks from Highsmith Company were the springboard for this theme. Based on them, she developed the lessons and activities for the year-long project. Wall displays related to the theme are clearly visible throughout the school library media center. Students in grades K–5 travel the world through the literature of different countries. Learning about the cultures of various nations is intended to enhance students' understanding of the diverse population at Colony Bend.

Susan has two links to the schoolwide goal. The first link is Tex, the Traveling Bear (see Photo 8.5, page 160). This cuddly bear in a red bandanna and cowboy hat carries a backpack or suitcase. He has a letter of introduction and a destination tag as well as a passport that is included in the check out. He is available to any students or parents whose trip takes them to a location outside the United States. All Susan asks is that Tex brings back to Colony Bend a photo or postcard from the travelers' destination and perhaps a small memento from the country (for example, a menu in the country's language, a brochure of sights, a foreign coin). Susan then uses these mementos and postcards to build a display in the school library media center that maps Tex's travels. Parents and students who would like to take Tex on a trip are asked to telephone or visit the library media center and inquire. Tex is an immensely popular learning tool that has been to such faraway places as England, Canada, Germany, and the Czech Republic.

Photo 8.5. As a major feature of Susan Link's "Book-a-Trip Around the World" program, parents and students are invited to check out Tex, the Traveling Bear, to take him on trips to locations outside the U.S. *(Colony Bend Elementary School, Sugar Land, Texas, Fort Bend Independent School District)*

Susan also links her school library media center to the overall goal in the school by relating learning centers to the fourth- and fifth-grade curriculum. For example, she may develop seven center activities for the fourth-grade study of Ireland, and seven others for the fifth-grade study of Australia. Through collaboration with the classroom teachers, Susan has arranged a schedule for the students to visit the various centers. Sample learning center activities related to Ireland include the following:

- SIRS Discoverer (CD-ROM): Finding specific information.
- Atlas (CD-ROM): Locating specific places.
- Flag Center: Drawing, coloring, and labeling the flag of Ireland.
- Encyclopedia: Using the encyclopedia to learn more about Ireland.
- Charting Weather Data Center: Using the newspaper weather section.
- Reading Center: Reading books about Ireland.
- People and Places: Finding information.

Susan mentions that once she develops the centers she can use the same center ideas for the other countries studied. She depends on the school newsletter to advertise these programs to teachers, students, and parents.

�֎ *Debby Stone, Fair-Oak Elementary School, Westminster, South Carolina, School District of Oconee*

"Virtual Field Trip Around the World with Katie"

This great program idea began when Debby's daughter, Katie, participated in an around-the-world voyage as a part of her college program. The ship planned to stop at 10 ports of call throughout the southern hemisphere. This experience led to a worldwide project sponsored by the school library media center that integrated all facets of the curriculum. Students in kindergarten through fifth grade were introduced to Katie during the weekly school news program broadcast from the media center. Digital photos of Katie, the ship, and the embarkation were imported into a PowerPoint presentation and presented on the news. A world map was displayed in the center along with a selection of nonfiction books on each country. Pins and yarn traced the route of the voyage. Students visited the Semester At Sea Web site for daily updates on the position of the ship.

Latitude and longitude points were plotted. All classes were invited to select one of the countries for a weekly broadcast news report. Typical items researched were landforms, economy, flags, monetary units, government, climate, clothing, and customs. Debby worked with groups on information searching, analysis, evaluation, and presentation. Students used a variety of reporting methods including PowerPoint, electronic books, speaking, travel brochure design, and newspaper reporting. Debby shared literature from each country or region with the students, and the music teacher concentrated on the musical style or instrumentation of the area. Students also had the opportunity to write letters or postcards. When Katie returned from the voyage, she visited the school to talk with students first-hand, share stories and souvenirs, and answer questions. Everyone in the school community became involved in sharing Katie's worldwide experience.

Sports and Cultures

✖ *Phyllis Mays, Code Elementary School, Seneca, South Carolina, School District of Oconee*

"*Code Olympic Day Extravaganza*" (This title is an acronym for Code Elementary School; each school can create its own acronym for its Olympic Day.)

This special program, which celebrates reading and also highlights Field Day (sports), can be done concurrently with the winter Olympics or in anticipation of an upcoming summer Olympics. Phyllis began by forming a committee of teachers (especially physical education teachers), the media specialist, and curriculum coordinator, who worked together to plan and execute this major extravaganza.

First, the team found and selected resource people to participate. They sent letters to parents and community members requesting that adults from foreign countries come and read to students. In the end, guests representing 23 foreign countries agreed to read and share multicultural activities. Guests and students were encouraged to wear the costumes of various countries.

The committee assigned each classroom in the school the task of drawing a flag from a specific country. Prior to the event, the colorful flags were hung outside each classroom. On event day, visitors representing various countries such as Egypt, China, Uganda, and Scotland went to the classroom displaying the flag representing his or her country. The visitors read a story related to the country to students in the classroom. Students were given a rotating schedule allowing them to visit five classrooms during the extravaganza; thus hearing five different stories and meeting five different visitors.

The cafeteria contributed to the event by preparing a lunch featuring foods from different countries. Tacos, fried rice, and pizza were served to students, guests, and teachers, who eagerly participated in the fun-filled event.

The highlight of the day focused on honoring the top readers in the school who were given gold medals. Then the Parade of Champion Readers began with the top reader in the school carrying a torch (unlit) through the building, while the other champion readers from each grade level followed, parading through the halls. The entire student body followed the parade to the playing field and opened the Olympic Field Day. This special Field Day, coordinated by the physical education teachers, began with a brief ceremony on that first day, with sporting events taking place the next.

Across the Curriculum

✖ *Donna Sullivan-Macdonald, Orchard School, South Burlington, Vermont, South Burlington School District*

"Focus on Thematic Units to Support Classroom Curriculum"

Integration of classroom thematic units and collaboration with classroom teachers play an important part in the design of library programming at Orchard School in South Burlington, Vermont. Whether it is a simple kindergarten story time or a content-rich second- and third-grade presentation and project, expansion of classroom themes is always a primary concern. Donna used a one-year-long thematic unit entitled "Hopping Through History" to illustrate second- and third-grade curriculum. Two of the six topics covered under this theme are detailed in Figure 8.1 to give an idea of how Donna supports and enriches the class curriculum through information, books, and activities.

Egyptians (four-week unit)

    A.   Pharaohs (crowns, crooks and flails)

    B.   Pyramids (jobs at a building site; types of pyramids)

    C.   Tut's Tomb

    D.   Communication (hieroglyphics, cartouches, papyrus)

    Books: *Tutankhamen's Gift* and *Pyramid*

    Projects: Making the double crown of Egypt, crooks, and flails

                  Papermaking

                  Three-dimensional pyramids with interior diagrammed cartouches of students' names

Medieval Times (seven-week unit)

    A.   Twelfth Night (including jobs at a Medieval Feast)

    B.   Castles—construction jobs, parts of a castle

    C.   Knighthood—steps in becoming a knight, armor parts

    D.   Illuminations and Stained Glass—the church, religious life

    E.   Village life—crafts, offense and defense of a castle

    F. Fairy tales

    Books: *Medieval Feast, Merry Ever After, Castles, Harold and the Giant Knight, Little Red Riding Hood, Rumplestiltskin*

    Projects: Recreating the Twelfth Night celebration

                  Constructing castles

                  Drawing coats of arms

                  Building houses for towns around castle

                  Assaulting castle—(battering rams, assault towers)

                  Making puppets for fairy tales

                  Playing medieval "Jeopardy" game

Figure 8.1. Sample thematic units to support curriculum areas.

Patty Williams, George Washington Elementary School, Kingsport, Tennessee, Kingsport City Schools

"A Thematic Approach"

In Kingsport, Tennessee the school selects a year-long theme, then decides on the components and key points needed to implement the curriculum. For example, "habitats" has been used as a theme to which each unit of study is tied. The school library media center supports this theme throughout the year by leading Internet searches, gathering resources, and helping students with research. Many teachers include a research component and the students come to the library media center regularly to research their topic using the print and nonprint materials available. Displays in the library also support the year-long theme. The displays include books and book jackets, realia, and student projects.

Social Studies and Science Tips

 Phyllis Mays, Code Elementary, Seneca, South Carolina, School District of Oconee

"Readers in Uniform"

Readers from various occupations are invited to visit the school in their appropriate uniforms. They read aloud to the students to illustrate how important reading is in the workplace. The books selected relate to their occupation. After reading, the guests discuss their jobs.

 Marilyn Mitchell, Mae Smythe Elementary, Pasadena Independent School District, Pasadena, Texas

"Museum Trunk Display"

Marilyn reminds media specialists that district professional libraries and museums sometimes have trunk collections that are available for check out. The trunks can be used to support the social studies program because they are often filled with items that focus on regional history or represent various cultures. Unfortunately, this service is often not advertised, so media specialists must contact area libraries and museums to inquire about what is available and then spread the word.

Personal Interests

Hobbies and Sports

"Wonderful World of Crafts"

To engage students in her planning process, one media specialist provides a suggestion box for students at the beginning of the school year. She posts a large sign asking for their ideas. When several suggestions indicated an interest in crafts, she developed "Wonderful Crafts" for School Library Week. Through her program, she was determined to attract students who showed little interest in using the library media center. She also aimed to acquaint students with various crafts.

Through a questionnaire to parents, she identified 12 speakers willing to share their unique craft talents. To add authenticity to the program and enhance student learning, she encouraged the volunteer speakers to bring their craft items at several stages of the creating process, and asked them to focus on demonstrating their crafts. Further, she encouraged them to bring instructional diagrams, when appropriate, and if possible, to offer some hands-on experiences for the children.

The media specialist divided her program into three crafts per day, never repeating a single craft throughout the four days. Teachers were given a schedule of events and invited to select an available time to bring their classes to the media center during the week. Throughout the media center, the media specialist displayed books relating to various crafts. Volunteers were available to provide support during the demonstrations. The media specialist set up separate demonstration areas in three corners of the library media center. Here the speakers offered a 10-minute demonstration of the following crafts:

Quilting	Macramé designing
Spinning	Weaving
Glass blowing	Silk screening
Easter egg painting	Sculpting
Pottery making	Wood carving
Woodworking	Model airplane building

The event was a tremendous success. Although logistically it was a challenge to single-handedly coordinate so many groups and volunteers, her rewards were many. She met her objectives and experienced a substantial increase in book circulation.

"Go One-on-One with a Star Athlete"

To entice the more reluctant readers, a Louisiana media specialist invited local sports figures to participate in a program with a sports theme. Professional, amateur, college, and high school athletic organizations provided excellent resources for locating participants. Although the most popular sports will interest young patrons, less-known sports can be just as exciting. Six sports figures volunteered to present information about their favorite sports:

- Baseball
- Soccer
- Basketball
- Hockey
- Cycling
- Gymnastics

In the weeks leading up to the event, the athletes were encouraged to bring sporting equipment, personal photographs and scrapbooks, posters, and information pamphlets about their sports to the media specialist, who then arranged displays and created space for the athletes to share their experiences and simulate demonstrations. The media specialist opened the festivities by inviting the entire student body to attend a presentation by the coach of a champion basketball team. Throughout the next two mornings, the athletes were available in the media center. Grade levels were scheduled, and teachers and students were invited to visit the library media center to hear the speakers, watch videos, ask questions, and get autographs.

Mary Lough, Margaret Beeks Elementary School, Blacksburg, Virginia, Montgomery County Public Schools

"Our Collections"

The entire school is invited to participate in this program that focuses on students' and teachers' collections. A laminated sign at the top front of the display case asks: "Do you have a collection to share?" A large sign reads "Our Collections."

The students (and sometimes teachers) sign up for a week on a sheet posted on the side of the display case. On Monday morning they bring their collection and set it up by themselves (and if necessary with help from a parent or a school mate). Mary has a laminated card stating "This collection of ______________________________ belongs to _____" that students fill in themselves. Because it is laminated, the card can be wiped clean and used repeatedly.

Some weeks Mary reserves the display case for her own collections or to publicize an event. Other weeks she reserves it for the occasional teachers willing to share an interesting collection. Generally, however, it is mostly students who do the exhibit.

Mary says, "The students really seem to enjoy seeing other people's collections. Beanie babies, rocks, dolls, arrowheads, and bears spark interest and help students learn about each other." It also provides students with ideas of collections they can begin themselves.

Also consider making a monthly display that showcases individual teachers or students with objects from their favorite hobbies. As always, display books relating to that hobby.

Humor

"Joke and Riddle Center"

Another elementary media specialist emphasizes higher-order thinking skills all year long by featuring a "Joke and Riddle Center" in her school library media center. Although the background information on jokes and riddles and her attractive signage introducing the center remain the same throughout the year, the focus of the center and the types of joke and riddle books change on a monthly basis. In February the learning center focused on "Knock Knock Jokes," and in March the focus was on "Elephant Jokes." Joke books were available in the center for students to become acquainted with the featured type of joke, and through carefully designed activities, children were encouraged to create their own jokes and place them into the attractive "Joke and Riddle Box" to share with other students in the school. (Riddles can also be the focus, with students developing their own riddles and providing the answers on the back for other students to enjoy.) This ongoing, year-long center provided teachers with an area of independent activities in the library media center to which they could send students.

Holidays and Special Events

Traditional Holidays

✱ *Bonnie Keith, Bales Intermediate School, Friendswood, Texas, Friendswood Independent School District*

"Great Pumpkin Events"

To introduce two events related to this theme, Bonnie sends all parents an announcement that includes the information in Figure 8.2, page 168:

GREAT PUMPKIN CHARACTER CONTEST

The library is sponsoring the Great Pumpkin Character Contest. At home, decorate a small pumpkin as your favorite book character, and bring the decorated pumpkin to the library media center.

Contest Rules:

- Decorate a small pumpkin as a character from a book found in the school library media center.

- Use materials like yarn, fabric scraps, magic markers, paint, cardboard, and glitter to create your character, but do not cut the pumpkin.

- Pumpkins that are carved will be disqualified.

- Each entry should have a 3- by 5- inch card attached with the character and title of the book written on one side, and the student's name, homeroom teacher, and grade written on the other.

- Pumpkins can be brought to the library beginning on (date).

- Judging will be on the morning of (date).

- Prizes will be awarded based on originality, creativity, and relevance to the book.

- Winners will receive gift certificates for books at our next book fair.

- Pumpkins can be picked up on (date).

- Any pumpkins that are left over will be discarded.

"Great Pumpkin Dress Up"

The principal wants to remind you that on (date) students can dress in costume (see Photo 8.6). Dress up as your favorite book character. Please follow these rules:

- No masks

- No blood and gore

- No violent accessories (guns, swords, knives)

- No costumes made of plastic bags

- Regular school dress code should be followed

Figure 8.2. Sample announcement of program contest and dress-up day.

Photo 8.6. Student with her Pippi Longstocking charac-
ter creation for "The Great Pumpkin Contest." (*Bales
Intermediate School, Friendswood, Texas, Friendswood
Independent School District*)

*Vicki Carter Broussard, Lake Arthur Elementary, Lake Arthur, Louisi-
ana, Jefferson Davis Parish Schools*

"Holiday Door Decorating Contest"

A door decorating contest prior to any holiday is always fun. The
school library media center distributes the rules and criteria for judging
to each classroom teacher. The door contest could focus on holiday books
and holiday book characters.

Vicki also suggested that media specialists ask each class to select a
favorite book related to Christmas, Halloween, Valentine's Day, Easter,
Hanukkah, and other holidays, then develop the door decorations
around that favorite book. Often the popularity of a specific book
becomes evident when numerous classrooms choose to focus on it. For
example, at one school *Polar Express* by Chris Van Allsburg was highlighted on eight classroom doors. (*Note:* This idea can also be tied to National Library Week or to a celebration of special community events such
as the local air show; the media specialist could decorate the door with
book jackets related to aviation, and all the classroom teachers can also
carry out the theme on their own doors.)

✠ *Suzanne Baxley, Brooklyn Springs Elementary, Lancaster, South Carolina, Lancaster County Schools*

"Easter Egg Scavenger Hunt"

This program lasts for four weeks and focuses on developing research skills. The media specialist makes question slips for students in the grade levels involved. The students choose Easter eggs out of a basket. Inside the eggs they find their reference questions. The eggs are numbered, and these are the numbers they put on their answer slips. Their reward for answering the questions correctly is a chocolate egg.

Birthday Celebrations

✠ *Phyllis Mays, Code Elementary School, Seneca, South Carolina, School District of Oconee*

"Birthday Book Club"

Each month, the library media specialist sends letters to students who have birthdays during that month. The students are invited to select and purchase a book for the library collection. A bookplate is placed in each book to honor the student's birthday.

✠ *Jay Stailey, Bales Intermediate School, Friendswood, Texas, Friendswood Independent School District*

"Birthday Club and the Principal"

Parents are offered an opportunity twice a year to select a gift book for the media center honoring his or her child. (A variety of titles are chosen by the media specialist, and the PTO helps to promote this event.) A bookplate honoring the child is placed in the book. Then Mr. Stailey, the principal, delivers the book selected for the birthday honoree to the child's classroom where he formally presents the book to the student. The birthday celebrant gets to read the book first, then the book becomes part of the collection. The program promotes reading and philanthropy, and it also gets the principal into the classroom.

✠ *Pam Kanoy, Pilot Elementary School, Thomasville, North Carolina, Guilford County Schools*

"Read Across America Celebrates Dr. Seuss's March 2 Birthday"

The entire school participates in the special national event, *Read Across America*, which is sponsored by the National Education Association. This event celebrates Dr. Seuss's birthday on March 2. NEA asks that every child in America read during the evening of March 2. Pam sends a letter home to parents describing the celebration activities and encouraging the parents to sit down with their child that evening and read.

Following are some of the special activities that Pam provides for students:

- Students in grades one through five read at least one Dr. Seuss book.

- One day is designated as "Red and White Day," on which everyone is encouraged to wear red and white.

- Students can bring a Dr. Seuss book from their home library to share with classmates.

- Students are asked to draw a picture of their favorite Dr. Seuss book or character.

- Pictures are displayed in the halls in the form of a birthday cake with a candle on top.

- Bookmarks and book covers are created.

- The cafeteria serves birthday cake on Friday at lunch.

- The third-grade teachers present a spelling unit based on Dr. Seuss.

- Students visit a Seuss Web site:
  www.randomhouse.com/seussville.

- The school principal, assistant principal, and a county administrator read books to classes.

- Students in grades one through five play "Dr. Seuss Bingo" with book titles.

❉ *Penny Hayne, Lake Murray Elementary, Chapin, South Carolina, School District Five of Lexington and Richland Counties*

"The Cat's Birthday"

Penny puts a different twist on *Read Across America*'s celebration of Dr. Seuss's March 2 birthday. Her school library media center hosts a birthday party for "The Cat in the Hat." Students make their own hats, play games, and enjoy a special cake that is decorated like the red and white hat that Dr. Seuss made famous. The students bring small gifts, such as crayons, stickers, and books, for the "Cat," who in turn donates them to a local shelter for homeless children.

Penny also sponsors a special program on Dr. Seuss's birthday for seniors in a local nursing home. She selects and invites a group of students to visit the nursing home and read to the senior citizens. Students' parents usually drive them to the home after school where the children read a Dr. Seuss book to the elderly on a one-on-one basis. Afterward, everyone enjoys a slice of birthday cake.

For more information on the *Read Across America* event in March, contact the National Education Association at 202-822-SEUS or at the Web site www.nea.org/readacross.

Special Days That Celebrate People and Books

"Grandparents' Day"

Send home an invitation to the parents and grandparents to attend a special production celebrating grandparents in the school library media center. On this invitation, also let them know that you will have books that can be purchased and donated to the library in honor of their special child or grandchild. Order about 50 new books on consignment from one of the publishers in the area and display these books.

On the day of the event, have parent volunteers encourage guests to purchase the books from the display as they enter the school. Also display sample bookplates from which guests can choose. Have a complete form available to provide the personalized messages they want on the bookplate. On the bottom of this form, add a receipt that they keep for proof of purchase (donations are tax deductible). Following the book sale, print the bookplates and glue them in the books. Let the honoree be the first to check out the book.

 Phyllis Mays, Code Elementary, Seneca, South Carolina, School District of Oconee

"Last Day of School" or "Graduation"

Throughout the school year, videotape the school's special activities. On the last day of school, show the special video. Dedicate a special section to the "graduating" fifth-grade students.

 Vicki Carter Broussard, Lake Arthur Elementary, Lake Arthur, Louisiana, Jefferson Davis Parish Schools

"Book Character Dress-Up Day and Parade of Floats"

Sponsor this special day through the library media center. Send home a letter to parents describing the event and discussing the rules. Students are invited to come to school dressed as a favorite book character. Encourage teachers to provide time in the morning for students to guess the characters. After lunch they are asked to wear a name tag that lists the character's name and title of the books. Grade levels are scheduled to visit the library for a 30-minute program related to special book characters.

For that special day, encourage each classroom to use a toy wagon to create a float related to a specific book. Invite all participating classes to join the "Parade of Floats" through the school building. After the exciting day, display the floats in the media center for the remainder of the month. Finally, provide a news release, with a photograph, to the local newspaper.

"Children's Book Week"

Take pictures of teachers reading their favorite children's book. Ask them to write a short paragraph that tells why they enjoyed reading it. Develop a bulletin board or display with this information. This activity can also be used during National Library Week.

Calendar of Events That Promote Libraries and Literacy

The American Library Association has an entire calendar of events to promote libraries and literacy. Some events that ALA promotes annually are:

January: National Book Month
   contact National Book Award
   212-685-0261 or www.nationalbook.org

March: Read Across America
   contact National Education Association
   202-822-SEUS or www.nea.org/readacross

April: School Library Media Month and National Library Week
   contact American Library Association
   800-545-2433, ext. 5041 or www.ala.org/pio

   Reading Is Fundamental
   contact Smithsonian Institution
   202-287-3220 or www.rif.org

September: International Literacy Day
   contact International Reading Association
   302-731-1600 or www.reading.org

   Banned Books Week
   contact American Library Association
   800-545-2433 or www.ala.org/bbooks/

November: Children's Book Week
   contact Children's Book Council
   212-966-1990 or www.cbcbooks.org

For complete information about the programs sponsored by ALA, telephone 1-800-545-2433 or access ALA's Web site at www.ala.org/events /promoevents. ALA can send you a packet filled with ideas for programs in your school library media center.

PROGRAMS FOR TEACHERS

Programs for teachers can be especially rewarding. Whether planned for inservice days, or before, during, or after school they enable you to support your colleagues and strengthen your professional relationships.

Promoting Reading Among Teachers

Betty Anne Smith, Royall Elementary School, Florence, South Carolina, Florence School District One

"Teachers as Readers"

Betty Anne has developed a successful professional development program for teachers based on a special program initiated by the International Reading Association. She sets up groups consisting of an administrator, teachers, and the media specialist. Each group is organized differently based on what works best for them. The group can meet as often as the members desire, and they can meet anywhere: in restaurants, parks, homes, or at school. Some groups meet monthly; Betty Anne's group meets five times a year in the school library media center. She serves refreshments and keeps the atmosphere informal.

Techniques for approaching this program can vary. Participants can all read the same book, different books by the same author, or different books on a special focus topic. After reading the book the group members share ideas, thoughts, and feelings as they respond to the literature. Some possible approaches are:

- The group members read different children's novels that are new to the library media center. During the session they have short discussions about how the books can be used in the classroom.

- The group members read the same children's book, and during the session they discuss the work.

- The group members read different picture books that are new to the school library media center. During the session they have short discussions about how they can be used in the classroom.

- The group focuses on a specific professional book to read and discuss.

Betty Anne provides the following tips that work for her:

- Purchase multiple copies with book fair proceeds, special budget appropriations through the principal, or with grant funds.
- Be sure to check with the International Reading Association about grants to defray the cost of books provided to participants.
- Place bookplates in the front of books given to teachers to read. State on the plate that the books were provided by the "Teachers as Readers Group."
- Occasionally invite a guest speaker to meet with the group. (Betty Anne has invited a book illustrator to discuss the illustration process and a representative from a bookstore to share new books.)
- When selecting books for the group to read, consider length, interest of topic, availability, and cost.
- Involve the school principal.

To obtain more detailed information on this program, contact the International Reading Association at 1-800-336-READ and ask for information about the "Teachers as Readers Group." There is a video and a starter kit (available for a fee).

Karen Czerwinski, Lulu M. Ross Elementary, Milford, Delaware, Milford School District

"Multicultural Literature Workshop"

Karen invites faculty to her school library media center for a special program on multicultural literature. She begins the session by asking the teachers to take a brief inventory of their current teaching practices by answering such questions as:

- Do you have a classroom library?
- Do you read aloud on a daily basis?
- Do you read literature with a variety of main characters?
- Do you read the same stories year after year?
- How often do you use books related to other cultures and ethnic groups?

A discussion of these questions often enlightens teachers about room for growth concerning the sharing of literature, particularly multicultural literature. Karen then shares some guidelines for selecting quality multi-cultural children's literature for the curriculum. (Guidelines can be found in children's literature textbooks listed under "Children's Literature" in Appendix E.) She discusses the quality selection tools, including journals such as *Booklist* and *Book Links* and lists of book awards such as the Coretta Scott King Book Award. She also provides teachers with an opportunity to browse various Web sites. Her favorite sites for teachers to visit are the following:

> *Vandergrift's Children's Literature Page*:
>   www.scils.rutgers.edu/special/kay/childlit.html
>
> *The Children's Literature Web Guide*
>   www.acs.ucalgary.ca/~dkbrown/authors.html

After the discussion, teachers browse the resources that are available to them in the school library media center. To facilitate this activity, Karen sets up displays of books and videos arranged by different geographical regions and subject content. For example, there may be a table display of folk literature from different countries around the world, Coretta Scott King Book Award winners, or books that focus on immigration. The resources are grouped so that they will be of the greatest interest to the teachers.

Karen receives much positive feedback about this program. It has been a successful professional development activity for the following reasons:

- It provides teachers with an opportunity to engage in meaningful discussion about a topic of great interest to them.

- It gives them an opportunity to browse the vast amount of multicultural resources that are readily available to them from the school library media center.

- It introduces them to some Internet Web sites.

- It encourages a working relationship with the library media specialist.

Mini-Workshops for Teachers

Susan Link, Colony Bend Elementary, Sugar Land, Texas, Fort Bend Independent School District

"The 20-Minute Workshop"

Mini-workshops or mini-programs can be designed to share interesting information with faculty in a short period of time. The key to successful programs is brevity: Programs should last about 20 minutes, and certainly no more than 30 minutes. Such programs allow media specialists to focus on a clearly defined skill or special interest of teachers and stimulate interest in the school library media center. Susan frequently uses this form of programming. She notes that following successful mini-workshops, book circulation among teachers increases significantly. Susan also reminds media specialists that because attendance should be voluntary, you may have only a small group of teachers at some of the workshops. Do not be disheartened by low attendance. Smaller groups genuinely excited about a topic can achieve much more than larger groups of only mildly interested participants.

Susan offers the following tips for planning successful mini-workshops:

- Schedule the program during a planning time for all faculty such as 3:00–3:30 p.m.

- Avoid interfering with after-school hours.

- Plan one meeting each month with focus topics and activities that vary.

- Make attendance at these workshops voluntary.

- At the beginning of the school year, ask faculty for suggestions concerning topics of interest.

- Plan ahead, and provide faculty with a calendar of events each semester.

"How to Create Story Aprons" (Appendix C)

Similar to a flannel board, a story apron can be used for sharing special children's books. Consider sharing a list of patterned or predictable books such as *Brown Bear, Brown Bear* and *The Very Hungry Caterpillar* with the teachers during the mini-workshop, as these books offer excellent story models around which to design the story aprons. Also provide teachers with samples of various story aprons that you have designed. Detailed instructions on creating and using story aprons are in Appendix C and in the following journal article:

> P. Wilson and S. Brown, "Creating Story Aprons for Library and Classroom Use," *School Library Media Activities Monthly*, 16, no. 3 (1999): 26–28.

"Topic Ideas for Teacher Workshops"

Media specialists from various schools provided the following topics that have been successfully implemented into the mini-workshop format.

Selection Aids. Many media specialists take for granted their own knowledge of the selection tools that they use to select outstanding books. You will find that many teachers are not aware of these professional resources, and they are often thrilled to learn about the selection aids available in the library media center. Include books such as *A to Zoo: Subject Access to Children's Picture Books* and *The Read-Aloud Handbook* as well as popular journals such as *Book Links.* You may also want to consider introducing them to some electronic selection aids.

Professional Journals. Introduce the teachers in your school to the professional journals at the elementary level. Because so few journals were available at her school, one creative media specialist asked the principal and each teacher in the school to bring a professional journal to the workshop to share with the other faculty members. The discussion also focused on electronic journals, and teachers were given an opportunity to examine several electronic journals such as the International Reading Association's *Reading Online* and *School Library Journal.* Faculty members left this short session with knowledge concerning the availability of journals beyond their own special areas of expertise.

New Resources in the Media Center. Take advantage of the opportunity to teach the teachers how to use new software and equipment available in the media center. Demonstrate and provide time for hands-on activities with a purpose.

Searching the Internet. Any number of topics can be the focus of this mini-workshop. Make it a fun, interesting, experience with plenty of hands-on opportunities. For example, the author Web sites in Chapter 6 could be the focus of an interesting workshop to familiarize teachers with resources offered on the Internet. Teachers will enjoy sharing these sites with their students. Other workshops could highlight the community resources also found in Chapter 6.

Using the Internet for Research. Share a variety of reference sources that can be found on the Internet. Emphasize the various search engines that are available. Ask teachers to bring a list of their favorite sites to share, and compile these into a handout for all who attended the session.

Publishers' Catalogs. Several library media specialists reported that teachers enjoyed learning about these catalogs that we take for granted. Because we often get duplicates of these catalogs, keep several on hand to give to all attendees as they leave the workshop.

Book Reviewing. This is another bit of knowledge many library media specialists take for granted. Teachers are very interested in hearing about the ways books are reviewed. Invite a reviewer (university professor or librarian who reviews children's or professional books for journals) to share information about the review process at a mini-workshop. Also bring in several review journals such as *Booklist*, *Horn Book*, *School Library Journal*, and *Book Links* for the teachers to become familiar with the review sources.

Book Fair Materials. Some media specialists arrange for their book fair company to provide a short program for faculty that focuses on the material available for the fair. This is usually done in the media center, and faculty are given an opportunity to browse the book fair without students present. Teachers also enjoy hearing about the selection process for the book fair. They welcome a list of the most popular books for children. Some media specialists arrange for the book fair to include professional materials for teachers and parents. During the mini-workshop, resources such as Judy Freeman's *More Books to Read Aloud* may be highlighted.

Children's Book Awards. Media specialists will find background information on these awards at various Web sites (see Chapter 6) as well as in children's literature textbooks, such as the ones recommended in Appendix E. Select the major awards, and provide teachers with a brief summary of their history and purpose. Make the most recent award-winning children's books available for faculty to enjoy. One media specialist noted: "Until the workshop, faculty were only familiar with the Newbery and Caldecott Awards. They were thrilled to learn about the Laura Ingalls Wilder Award and the Orbis Pictus Award."

Reading Aloud. A workshop for teachers on the importance of reading aloud is usually well received by faculty. At the workshop, share tips on reading aloud and familiarize faculty with resources such as Jim Trelease's *Read Aloud Handbook* and Judy Freeman's *Books Kids Will Sit Still For*, which recommend titles of good books to read aloud. One media specialist who offered this mini-program commented: "The teachers in my school were excited to learn about the professional books that list specific titles of children's books to use as read-alouds. I also plan to offer the program for parents." (See Appendix D for more related titles.)

Bookstores. Invite an owner or a representative of a local bookstore to your school library media center to share information with teachers. For example, at one mini-session a bookstore owner shared a list of the "Best Selling Children's Books of the Year" with teachers. She also brought along copies and presented booktalks on three of the most popular adult novels.

Luncheons, Receptions, Breakfasts. Numerous media specialists across the nation indicated that faculty interest in the media center increased after inviting them to programs and activities in the library media center. Brown-bag luncheons, economical receptions with punch and cookies, and light breakfasts of rolls and coffee were just a few of the events library media specialists used to capture the teachers' interest in the media center. To add a professional development component to the event, showcase new professional and children's books.

Field Trip Experiences. Offer field trips after school to special library-related sites such as the district level professional resources library, a local bookstore, or a nearby university.

What's New in the Media Center

The contributors for our book suggested the following ways to advertise the professional and student resources available in the library media center:

- Make banners and place them on the inside of the faculty restroom stalls. Everyone has to go to the restroom some time during the day, and now you have a captive audience.

- Prior to faculty meetings, display new library materials for faculty to examine before or after the meeting. Several media specialists were pleasantly surprised that teachers sometimes arrived early to browse through the materials.

- Ask the principal to provide a five-minute period at the beginning of faculty meetings for you to advertise new materials.

- Highlight new materials in a special section of the school or media center newsletter.

- Display new professional materials in the teachers' lounge.

- Use a cart for the rolling display of "New Arrivals" in the teacher's lounge.

- Develop a creative "New Arrivals" memo, and send notes to teachers.

- Display titles of new professional materials on a bulletin board in the teachers' lounge.

- Take the new materials of interest to grade-level meetings and share them with faculty.

PROGRAMS FOR PARENTS

Programs make excellent vehicles for involving parents in their children's learning. Consider different approaches. Some programs solely target parents. They can either share information related to students (reference resources for choosing great children's books) or be directed exclusively to them (Internet search for beginners). Others are designed for parents and individual children (a father/daughter reception) or for entire families (reading together). Parents appreciate being included. Hosting programs for them meets that need, and enhances your reputation in the community.

Reaching Out to Families

❋ *Suzanne Baxley, Brooklyn Springs Elementary School, Lancaster, South Carolina, Lancaster County Schools*

"Baby Beavers Book Club"

This marvelous program targets parents and newborns and continues throughout the school year. Send a letter to parents in the school asking them to contact the media specialist if they have a new baby during the school year. Suzanne lets the parents know that the school library media center wants to honor "our newest beavers" by sending a special gift. Her letter appears in Figure 8.3.

BABY BEAVERS LOVE TO READ TOO CLUB

Congratulations on your new baby. We would like to honor our newest beavers by sending you a special gift that we hope will help your new child learn to love reading at an early age. If you have a new baby this school year, please let us know. *(They are then asked to complete an attached form and have the baby's brother or sister bring it to the library media center.)*

Figure 8.3. Sample letter to parents.

When the parents of new babies do complete the form, the baby becomes a member of the "Baby Beavers Book Club" and receives a gift packet from the library media center that includes a picture frame for a first picture, a bookmark, a pencil, a book the family can read to the baby, and a list of recommended books that the whole family might enjoy. The parents are also notified that a book has been placed in the Brooklyn Springs Library Media Center in the child's honor. A letter to the baby states: "Your parents are welcome to come to our library and check this book out to share with you and your family. The title of the book is: _____."

The success of this program depends on the news of the program getting out to parents. Therefore, Suzanne advertises this program in the following ways: (1) sends information to parents in a letter, (2) meets with kindergarten parents at orientation, and (3) gives a newsletter to parents at PTA Open House.

Suzanne says the program is relatively inexpensive because the book in honor of the "baby beaver" comes from books she has already ordered for the regular collection. She just places a plate in the book with the baby's name when the parent comes to check it out. For the gift packet, she uses items with the school logo, stickers, bookmarks, and a paperback that was purchased at the book fair. Funding comes from the book fair and the principal's budget. By reaching out to parents in this simple and kind way, Suzanne creates outstanding PR for her media center.

�֎ *Suzanne Baxley, Brooklyn Springs Elementary, Lancaster County Schools, Lancaster, South Carolina*

"Adult Eager Beaver Readers"

This ongoing activity targeted at parents and other members of the community is done in conjunction with the previous program. Flyers are sent to parents, announcements are made at PTA Open House, and the media specialist advertises it when she meets with kindergarten parents at orientation. Suzanne's flyer appears in Figure 8.4.

Suzanne sponsors a special "kick off" activity for the annual open house in the school library media center. She serves refreshments and asks guests to sign up to become new members of the Brooklyn Springs Community Library. Her advertisements reads: WANTED: ADULT EAGER BEAVER READERS!

The faculty and staff of Brooklyn Springs strongly believe that if you read to your child, your child will become a good reader and a good listener. Since reading is such an important part of our curriculum, we invite you to come to our library and check out books that you can read to your children at home.

You are welcome at any time during the day. You can check out up to seven books weekly. During our annual Open House at the beginning of each school year, we hold a special sign-up night. We hope you will come in and fill out a short information form which allows us to put your name in our computer system. We are looking forward to having your child as a student next year, and we will do everything we can to help him/her have a wonderful first year at school.

Figure 8.4. Sample flyer announcing ongoing program.

Susan Link Colony Bend Elementary, Sugar Land, Texas, Fort Bend Independent School District

"*Read to Me* Literacy Kits"

Parents of students in grades K–2 were constantly requesting books at their child's reading level that they could use at home. Recognizing the need for more books in the library media center to serve this purpose, Susan applied for and received a grant from her school district to fund this wonderful parent outreach program. (Consider, also, submitting proposals to local service groups such as the Rotary or Lions Club.)

The major focus of this program involves providing parents with *Read to Me* Literacy Kits that encourage parents to read to and with their children at home. The kits (1) provide books for students to read orally to improve reading ability and summarization skills, and (2) provide books on the same theme for parents to read aloud to their child to foster a love of reading. The kits were designated for K–2 parents to check out from the school's library for use at home. Kits can also be used by older siblings to "buddy read" to younger brothers and sisters.

Susan and parent volunteers developed the kits, which consist of plastic storage boxes that contain the following:

- Books at a designated reading level on a related theme for students

- Storybooks for parents to read aloud to their child

- A puppet, character doll, or character of a stuffed animal

Once the kits were available for parent check out, Susan advertised the program to parents by (1) writing an article in the school newsletter, *The Pony Express,* (2) demonstrating the kits at a PTO Meeting, and (3) promoting them during K–2 class visits to the school library media center.

To get feedback on the kits and to give parents and students an opportunity to respond, each kit has a journal of its own and bookmarks for the parent and child. The journal stays with the kit. Figure 8.5 shows examples of journal entries.

Student's entry: "The books were nice. I read one book to my little sister. Then some nights my mom and sister and me all took turns reading. It was fun. Thank you for the bookmarks."

Parent entry: "I think these reading kits are really great! Kelli enjoyed having the books read to her and playing (acting out) with the dolls. I wish there were more kits for her grade level. Thanks."

Parent entry: "We really enjoyed the 'Grandmother Kit.' Since our grandmothers are from Greece and our cousin's grandmother is from Russia, this unit really hit home."

Figure 8.5. Sample journal entries.

For media specialists interested in developing the kits, Susan provides the following sample list shown in Figure 8.6.

Theme: Grandmothers

Reading Level K

Storage Box contains:

      Strega Nona doll

Books:

      Too Many Babas

      A Kiss for Little Bear

      Thunder Cake

      Strega Nona

Theme: Humor

Reading Level 1

Storage box contains:

      If You Give a Mouse a Cookie doll

Books:

      Amelia Bedelia

      Thank You, Amelia Bedelia

      If You Give a Mouse a Cookie

      There Is a Carrot in My Ear and Other Noodle Tales

Figure 8.6. Sample items for literacy kits.

More Ways to Advertise the Media Center

- Designate a small area of your library or workroom shelf for parents. In this section of the school library media center, house educationally related books that parents would find interesting.

- Hold a mini-workshop for parents on "Selection Aids: Keys to Good Reading." During this 20-30 minute session, introduce resources such as Jim Trelease's *Read Aloud Handbook* or Donna Norton's *Through the Eyes of a Child* that can help parents select good books for their children.

- Hold a reception at the beginning of the school year for parents who may be interested in volunteering in your school library media center.

- Hold a reception each month for parents from the various grade levels. For example, in September parents of kindergarten students may be eager to attend a reception in their honor and learn more about the school library media center and meet the media specialist. In October parents of first-graders may enjoy hearing about the benefits of reading aloud.

- Speak once or twice a year to parents at PTA or PTO meetings. Let members know about all the exciting programs and activities that you have going on in the school library media center. Share resources that can be found in the school library media center. This may be a good time to request volunteers to read aloud or offer presentations at special programs. Bring along your community resources questionnaire for them to complete (see figure 5.1).

CONCLUSION

To create each of these outstanding programs, the contributing media specialists matched their unique talents and expertise to the needs and interest of students, school, and community. Although you are welcome to use these programs as written, we encourage you to create original events as well. Either way, incorporate programs whenever possible. They can truly be the lifeblood of your library media center.

National Survey of School Library Programming

1. How many "school library programs"* have you provided this school year? _____ (if retired, or no longer serving as a library media specialist, how many programs did you provide during your final year? _____)

2. Upon which of the subject areas listed below do your library programs most frequently focus (please check *one*):

   ___ Reading/literature/language arts/English
   ___ Personal interests of students
   ___ Curriculum beyond English/language arts
   ___ Professional development for teachers
   ___ Computer technology

   Other _____

3. How often do you call on community resources (people, places, or things within your community) to support your programs?

   _____ often _____ sometimes _____ seldom _____ never

   Name a community resource you recently integrated into a program:

   _____

*Definition of school library program: a special event planned by the media specialist. This event may take place at a site other than the library media center.

4. What is the biggest problem you face when planning and presenting library programs?

5. Do your library programs serve as a form of public relations? Please comment.

6. Do you collaborate with teachers when developing library programs? Please comment.

7. What is the major reward derived from developing a library program? List other benefits derived.

8. How does your principal feel about special events in the library media center?

9. How do you most often gain financial support for library programs?

10. Write a statement that answers the following: Why do you feel library programs are important?

Sue Wiley's Sample Library Program Plan

Topic: Rodeos and Cowboys: Today and Yesterday
(The school library media center will sponsor a variety of programs throughout one month that are tied to the topic.)

Culminating Event: Guest speaker, a former rodeo competitor, shares his rodeo adventures with fourth-grade students and faculty.

Target Group: Fourth graders

Time: One hour

Location: Sue Wiley's School Library Media Center

Goals:
1. To familiarize students with materials in the school library media center that focus on cowboys and rodeos.

2. To share information with students about rodeos and cowboys of today and the past.

3. To share with students the activities that go on behind the scenes at the rodeo.

4. To tie school activities to a major community event.

Materials:
1. Microphone for guest speaker

2. Books related to rodeos for displays

3. Display table (for items brought by guest speaker)

Procedures:
1. Volunteers greet and seat students and faculty (monitor traffic flow).

2. Volunteers are assigned to take care of lights and sound.

3. Introduce guest speaker.

4. The speaker talks to students and demonstrates rodeo techniques.

5. A question-and-answer session takes place.

6. Concluding remarks are made by the media specialist, who invites everyone to the school library media center throughout the week to participate in exhibits, displays, and learning centers.

7. Volunteers monitor traffic flow as students return to classrooms.

Ancillary Programs:
1. Exhibit of items related to rodeos (provided by a faculty member)

2. Chuckwagon cooking demonstration (guest demonstrates making beef jerky)

3. Book and rodeo art displays

4. Learning centers related to topic (classroom teachers and media specialist collaborate)

5. Video on the history of the local rodeo

Publicity:
1. Write a brief article for the school newspaper that describes the upcoming event.

2. Send a letter home to parents of students describing the upcoming event.

3. Contact the newspaper and invite a reporter to the upcoming event.

4. Following the event, send a photograph and article about the event to the local newspaper.

5. Send a final report to the administration of school district describing the success of the event.

Follow-up Activities:
1. Related books will be exhibited in the library media center for the remainder of the month.

2. Learning centers related to the topic will be available in the library media center.

3. Reference materials on the topic will be highlighted in the school library media center.

4. Teachers will be encouraged to develop classroom learning centers.

5. The media specialist will provide teachers with a list of suggested classroom projects related to the topic.

6. The media specialist will provide teachers with a bibliography of resources (including Internet addresses) related to the topic.

Follow-up Correspondence and Acknowledgments:
1. The media specialist will send a handwritten thank-you to the speaker and other guests who participated in the various events.

2. The principal will send a letter of appreciation to the speaker and other guests who participated in the various events.

3. Students will be encouraged to send thank-yous.

4. Volunteers will be honored with a thank-you coffee.

Evaluation of Program:
1. Book circulation data

2. Informal student and faculty comments

3. Formal evaluation forms for students and faculty

4. Overall school library media usage by students and faculty

Appendix **C**

Library Media Activities

CREATING AND USING STORY APRONS

Story aprons are used by teachers and librarians to enrich storytelling or reading aloud. They are used in a manner similar to a flannel board. Illustrations or three-dimensional objects representing the setting, characters, and objects are attached to the apron as the story is read or told. The aprons clarify the sense of the story, its characters, setting, and plot. Thus, they enhance a child's understanding of a story and promote a love of reading.

Although most picture books can be adapted to story apron activities, predictable or patterned books such as Laura Numeroff's *If You Give a Mouse a Cookie* and Bill Martin's *Brown Bear, Brown Bear* serve as ideal springboards for story aprons. The repeated phrases, rhymes, or other patterns in these picture books help youngsters predict as they read the story. Using these predictable books, teachers find that the repetition simplifies the story. Many of the popular predictable books can also be found in the oversized book format typically referred to as "big books." These are particularly useful during story apron activities.

Story aprons vary according to the creativity of the designer. Choosing just the right type of apron for the specific book is an important consideration. Creative teachers who enjoy sewing and designing can create their own aprons; others may purchase the ready-made product from a kitchen or craft store. Kitchen aprons, barbecue aprons, chef's aprons, and carpenter's aprons all work well for this project. The type of apron to select may reflect the theme of the book. For example, use a chef's apron for a story about delectable foods. Similarly, use a carpenter's apron for developing an activity about tools and carpentry.

The development of the items related to the story such as the characters, setting, and specific objects depends on the creativity of the individual. A media specialist may want to design his or her own items for the apron; others may choose to purchase the items from a store and adapt them for apron use. A variety of products can be used to attach the items to the apron. Flannel works well for light-weight, flat objects. Others find that Velcro or magnetic strips meet their special needs. The manipulation of the items is critical to the story, because as the teacher or student reads the story aloud, the appropriate items must be attached.

A special container for storing the apron further enriches the activity. Containers such as decorated boxes, envelopes, or special folders that include the name of the author and book title provide simple ways to protect and organize story aprons. Other media specialists enjoy using more creative containers such as a basket or a lunch box that may reflect the theme of the book.

Story apron activities typically consist of the following parts:

1. Children's trade book (predictable book is recommended) or folklore.

2. Apron (background on which to place objects).

3. Title of story and author (may be printed anywhere on the apron or may be placed somewhere near the story apron presentation).

4. Objects related to the story that will be placed on apron (characters, setting, various items mentioned in story).

5. A container (used to store the apron and the individual pieces).

A photograph of a sample story apron is shown in Chapter 4. For more information on the development of story aprons, the following article provides detailed instructions:

Wilson, Patricia, and Suzanne Brown. 1999. Creating story aprons for library and classroom use. *School Library Media Activities Monthly*, 16 (3): 26-28.

CREATING JACKDAWS

The term jackdaw usually refers to portfolios of materials (photographs, documents, maps, letters, speeches) that focus on a specific informational topic (a particular Civil War battle, the Declaration of Independence), or a famous person (Abraham Lincoln or George Washington). Jackdaws are developed with the intent of bringing a particular period of history to life for students. Middle school and high school media specialists often purchase these supplementary resources from commercial companies that specialize in the development of jackdaws. They are then offered to students and teachers for checkout.

Elementary media specialists can carry this idea one step further by developing jackdaw units that would be of interest to elementary youngsters. These could focus on topics related to informational books, biographies, and historical fiction. Once the documents are selected and developed for the portfolio or box, the media specialist identifies books in the media center to pair with the documents. In this way, the setting and people in the books become more real to the students.

Some media specialists carry this idea even further by encouraging students to develop jackdaws after reading informational or historical fiction books. Sample jackdaws are shared and students are asked to select one or two books on a particular topic. Then they design and create their very own jackdaws that are shared through displays in the library media center. (*Note*: Students may be encouraged to develop jackdaws that contain actual three-dimensional objects that relate to the topic. Additionally, they can develop a container based on the theme to hold the items. Student-made jackdaws provide wonderful displays for the school library media center.)

Appendix **D**

Resources to Support Special Programs

AUTHOR VISITS

Buzzeo. Toni. 1998. The finely tuned author visit. *Book Links* 7 (4): 10–15.

Buzzeo, Toni, and Jane Kurtz. 1999. *Terrific connections with authors, illustrators, and storytellers.* Englewood, CO: Libraries Unlimited.

East, Kathy. 1995. *Inviting children's authors and illustrators: A how-to-do-it manual for school and public librarians.* no. 49. New York: Neal-Schumann.

Schwartz, David M. 1995. Make every author visit a smashing success. *Instructor* 104 (7): 48–51.

Watkins, Jan. 1996. *Programming author visits.* Chicago: American Library Association.

(Note: Also see the Internet sites for children's authors listed in Chapter 6. The sites provide numerous tips concerning successful author visits.)

INFORMATION ABOUT AUTHORS

Berger, Laura Standley, ed. 1995. *Twentieth century children's writers.* 4th ed. Detroit: St. James Press.

Book Links. 1991. Chicago, IL: American Library Association.

Collier, Laurie, and Joyce Nakamura, eds. 1992. *Major authors & illustrators for children and young adults.* Detroit: Gale Research. (6 volumes)

Hotze, Ally Holmes. 1996. *Seventh book of junior authors and illustrators.* New York: H. W. Wilson.

McElmeel, Sharron. 1990. *An author a month (for nickels)*. Englewood, CO: Libraries Unlimited.

———. 1988. *An author a month (for pennies)*. Englewood, CO: Libraries Unlimited.

Silvey, Anita, ed. 1995. *Children's books and their creators*. Boston: Houghton Mifflin.

Something About the Author. 1971– . Detroit: Gale Research. (multi-volume set)

Teacher Librarian. Seattle, WA: Rockland Press. (Formerly *Emergency Librarian*, begun in 1973.)

(Note: Also see Internet sites listed in Chapter 6 for authors. They provide valuable information on the life and works of various children's authors.)

BOOKTALKING PROGRAMS

Baxter, Kathleen A., and Marcia Agness Kochel. 1999. *Gotcha! Nonfiction booktalks to get kids excited about reading*. Englewood, CO: Libraries Unlimited.

Bodart, Joni Richards. 1997. *Booktalking the award winners 4*. New York: H. W. Wilson.

Gillespie, John T., and Corinne J. Naden. 1994. *Middleplots 4: A book talk guide for use with readers ages 8–12*. New Providence, NJ: R. R. Bowker.

Thomas, Rebecca L. 1993. *Primary plots 2: A book talk guide for use with readers ages 4–8*. New Providence, NJ: R. R. Bowker.

READ-ALOUD PROGRAMS

Bauer, Caroline Feller. 1985. *Celebrations: Read-aloud holiday and theme book programs*. New York: H. W. Wilson Company.

———. 1987. *Presenting reader's theater: Plays and poems to read aloud*. New York: H. W. Wilson.

Freeman, Judy. 1990. *Books kids will sit still for*. New York: R. R. Bowker.

———. 1995. *More books kids will sit still for*. New York: R. R. Bowker.

Trelease, Jim. 1997. *The read-aloud handbook*. 4th ed. New York: Penguin.

STORYTELLING AND DRAMA

Bauer, Caroline Feller. 1997. *Leading kids to books through puppets*. Chicago: American Library Association.

Champlin, Connie. 1998. *Storytelling with puppets*. Chicago: American Library Association.

Geisler, Harlynne. 1997. *Storytelling professionally*. Englewood, CO: Libraries Unlimited.

Knowles, Elizabeth, and Martha Smith. 1997. *The reading connection: Bringing parents, teachers, and librarians together*. Englewood, CO: Libraries Unlimited.

Norton, Terry L., and Carol S. Anfin. 1996. Let's celebrate: Holiday storytelling with visual aids. *School Library Media Activities Monthly* 13 (4): 23–25.

Picone, Betty Ann. 1998. A reading camp in: How and why you should try hosting one. *School Library Media Activities Monthly* 14 (10): 22–23, 30.

Selected Topical Bibliography

CHILDREN'S LITERATURE

Bauer, Caroline Feller. 1983. *This way to books*. New York: H. W. Wilson.

———. 1992. *Read for the fun of it: Active programming with books for children*. New York: H. W. Wilson.

———. 2000. *Leading kids to books through magic*. Chicago: American Library Association.

Book Links. 1991. Chicago: American Library Association.

Cianciolo, Patricia J. 2000. *Informational picture book for children*. Chicago: American Library Association.

Cullinan, Bernice, and Lee Galda. 1994. *Literature & the child*. 3d ed. Orlando: Harcourt Brace.

Fredericks, Anthony D. 1997. *The librarian's complete guide to involving parents through children's literature, grades K–6*. Englewood, CO: Libraries Unlimited.

Freeman, Evelyn B., and Diane Goetz Person. 1998. *Connecting informational children's books with content area learning*. Boston: Allyn & Bacon.

Huck, Charlotte, Susan Hepler, Janet Hickman, and Barbara Z. Kiefer. 1997. *Children's literature in elementary school*. 6th ed. Boston: McGraw-Hill.

Johst, Lee Ann Lannom. 1995. *The use of multicultural trade books in the elementary curriculum*. Albany, New York: State University of New York Press.

Larrick, Nancy. 1991. *Let's do a poem: Introducing poetry to children*. New York: Delacorte Press.

Lukens, Rebecca J. 1999. *A critical handbook of children's literature*. 6th ed. Reading, MA: Addison-Wesley Longman.

Norton, Donna E. 1999. *Through the eyes of a child: An introduction to children's literature*. 5th ed. Upper Saddle River, NJ: Merrill.

Raines, Shirley C. 1994. *450 more story stretchers for the primary grades: Activities to expand children's favorite books*. Beltsville, MD: Gryphon House.

COPYRIGHT

Bruwelheide, Janis H. 1995. *Copyright primer for librarians and educators*. 2d ed. Chicago: American Library Association.

Heinich, Robert, Michael Molenda, James D. Russell, and Sharon E. Amaldino. 1999. *Instructional media and technology for learning*. 6th ed. Upper Saddle River, NJ: Merrill.

Samuels, Jeffrey M. 1999. *Patent, trademark, and copyright laws 1999*. Washington, DC: BNA Books.

Simpson, Carol Mann. 1997. *Copyright for the schools: A practical guide*. Worthington, OH: Linworth.

DISPLAYS AND EXHIBITS

Durbin, Gail. 1996. *Developing museum exhibitions for lifelong learning*. Lanham, MD: The Stationery Office.

Hawthorne, Karen, and Jane Gibson. 1999. *Bulletin boards and 3-D showcases that capture them with pizzazz*. Englewood, CO: Libraries Unlimited.

Menard, Christine. 1995. *More bright & bold bulletin boards*. Fort Atkinson, WI: Alleyside Press.

Roberts, Lisa C. 1997. *From knowledge to narrative: Educators and the changing museum*. Washington, DC: Smithsonian Institution Press.

Schaeffer, Mark. 1991. *Library displays handbook*. New York: H. W. Wilson.

Tedeschi, Anne C., et al.. 1997. *Book displays: A library exhibits handbook*. Highsmith Press Handbook Series. Fort Atkinson, WI: Highsmith Press.

EVENTS/PROGRAMMING

Barron, Daniel D. 1995. School library media programs: Prescription for the 21st century. *School Library Media Activities Monthly* 12 (1): 48–50.

Kimzey, Ann C., Patricia Wilson, Linda Garner. 1984. School library programming with community resources. *Top of the News* (Fall): 89–92.

Knowles, Elizabeth, and Martha Smith. 1997. *The reading connection: Bringing parents, teachers, and librarians together.* Englewood, CO: Libraries Unlimited.

Marks, Diana. F. 1998. *Let's celebrate today: Calendars, events and holidays.* Englewood, CO: Libraries Unlimited.

Picone, Betty Ann. 1998. A reading camp in: How and why you should try hosting one. *School Library Media Activities Monthly* 14 (10): 22–23, 30.

Sinofsky, Esther R. 1995. Doing the hustle: Public relations. *School Library Media Activities Monthly* 11 (5): 31, 42.

LEARNING CENTERS

Gayeski, Diane M., ed. 1995. *Designing communication and learning environments.* Englewood Cliffs, NJ: Educational Technology Publications.

Houle, Georgia Bradley. 1997. *Learning centers for young children: To be built in classrooms and other places where children gather to learn.* West Greenwich, RI: Consortium.

Ingrahm, Phoebe Bell. 1997. *Creating & managing learner centers: A thematic approach.* ED404024.

Isbell, Rebecca. 1995. *The complete learning center book: An illustrated guide for 32 different early childhood learning centers.* Beltsville, MD: Gryphon House.

McClay, Jodi. 1997. *Learning centers.* Westminster, CA: Teacher Created Materials.

Rice, Donna Herweck. 1997. *How to manage learning centers in the classroom: Grades K–6.* Westminster, CA: Teacher Created Materials.

Sykes, Judith A. 1997. *Library centers.* Englewood, CO: Libraries Unlimited.

PUBLIC RELATIONS

Flowers, Helen F. 1998. *Public relations for school library media programs: 500 ways to influence people and win friends for your school library media center*. New York: Neal-Schuman.

Karp, Rashelle S. 1995. *Part-time public relations with full-time results: A PR primer for libraries*. Chicago: American Library Association.

McPartland, Donna. 1995. Selling your library media program. *School Library Media Activities Monthly* 11 (10): 28–29.

Robinson, David E. 1996. Energizing the library media center. *School Library Media Activities Monthly* 12 (5): 24–27.

Valenza, Joyce Kasman. 1998. *Power tools: 100+ essential forms and presentations for your school library information program*. Chicago: American Library Association.

Wiltsee, Denise R., and Ella Marie Yates. 1998. Savvy selling solutions for the school media center. *Computers in Libraries* 18 (8): 36–38.

Wolfe, Lisa A. 1997. *Library public relations, promotions, and communications: A how-to-do-it manual*. How-to-do-it Manuals for Librarians, no. 75. New York: Neal-Schuman.

TECHNOLOGY

Anderson, Glenn. 1996. Setting up computer workstations in classrooms and libraries. *Media & Methods* 32 (5): 14, 16.

The directory of video, multimedia & audio-visual products 1997–98 (Serial). 1997. Mountain View, CA: Daniels.

Heinich, Robert, Michael Molenda, James D. Russell, and Sharon E. Amaldino. 1999. *Instructional media and technology for learning*. 6th ed. Upper Saddle River, NJ: Merrill.

MacDonald, Randall M. 1997. *The internet and the school library media specialist: Transforming traditional services*. Greenwood Professional Guides in School Librarianship. Westport, CT: Greenwood Press.

Miller, Elizabeth B. 1998. *The internet resource directory for K–12 teachers and librarians*. 97/98 ed. Englewood, CO: Libraries Unlimited.

Newby, Timothy J., et al. 1999. *Instructional technology for teaching and learning: Designing instruction, integrating computers, and using media*. 2d ed. Paramus, NJ: Prentice-Hall.

Roblyer, M. D., and Jack Edwards. 1999. *Integrating educational technology into teaching.* Upper Saddle River, NJ: Merrill.

Simpson, Carol Mann. 1995. *Internet for library media specialists.* Worthington, OH: Linworth.

Simpson, Carol, and Sharron L. McElmeel. 1997. *Internet for schools.* 2d ed. Worthington, OH: Linworth.

Small, Ruth V., and Marilyn P. Arnone. 1999. Web site quality: Do students know it when they see it? *School Library Media Activities Monthly* 15 (6): 25–26, 30.

Truett, Carol, et al. 1997. Responsible internet use. *Learning and Leading with Technology* 24 (6): 52–55.

VOLUNTEERS

Anderson, Mary Alice. 1999. Finding time. *Multimedia Schools* 6 (1): 26–28.

Bard, Therese Bissen. 1999. *Student assistants in the school library media center.* Englewood, CO: Libraries Unlimited.

Harada, Violet H., and Joan Yoshina. 1996. Parents as research mentors. *School Library Media Activities Monthly* 13 (4): 26–27.

McCune, Bonnie F., and Charleszine Nelson. 1995. *Recruiting and managing volunteers in libraries: A how-to-do-it manual.* How-to-do-it Manual for Librarians, no. 51. New York: Neal-Schuman.

Sherman, Gale W. 1998. How one library solved the overcrowded storytime problem. *School Library Journal* 44 (11): 36–38.

References

Aliki. 1983. *A medieval feast*. New York: Thomas Y. Crowell.

Barett, Judi, 1978. *Cloudy with a chance of meatballs*. New York: Atheneum.

Booklist. 1905. Chicago: American Library Association.

Burnett, Frances Hodgson. 1962. *The secret garden*. Illustrated by Tasha Tudor. Philadephia: J. B. Lippincott.

Calmenson, Stephanie. 1989. *The principal's new clothes*. Illustrated by Denise Brunkus. New York: Scholastic.

Carle, Eric. 1979. *The very hungry caterpillar*. New York: Philomel.

Carrick, Donald. 1982. *Harold and the giant knight*. New York: Clarion Books.

Coerr, Eleanor. 1993. *Sadako and the thousand paper cranes*. Illustrated by Ed Young. New York: Putnam.

Croll, Carolyn. 1994. *Too many babas*. New York: HarperCollins.

dePaola, Tomie. 1997. *Strega Nona*. New York: Simon & Schuster.

Freeman, Judy. 1990. *Books kids will sit still for*. New York: R. R. Bowker.

———. 1995. *More books kids will sit still for*. New Providence, NJ: R. R. Bowker.

Horn Book Magazine. 1926. Boston: Horn Book.

Hyman, Trina Schart. 1983. *Little Red Riding Hood*. New York: Holiday House.

Lasker, Joe. 1976. *Merry ever after*. New York: Viking Press.

Lima, Sharon, and John Lima. 1998. *A to Zoo: Subject access to children's picture books*. New Providence, RI: R. R. Bowker.

Macaulay, David. 1975. *Pyramid*. Boston: Houghton Mifflin.

———. 1977. *Castle*. Boston: Houghton Mifflin.

Major authors and illustrators. 1993– . 6-volume set. Detroit: Gale Research.

Martin, Bill. 1967. *Brown bear, brown bear*. Illustrated by Eric Carle. New York: Holt, Rinehart & Winston.

Martin, Bill, and John Archambault. 1986. *Barn dance*. Illustrated by Ted Rand. New York: Henry Holt.

Minarik, Else. 1984. *A kiss for little bear*. Illustrated by Maurice Sendak. New York: Harper & Row.

Montgomery, L. M. 1989. *Anne of Green Gables*. Illustrated by Lauren Mills. Boston: Godine.

Norton, Donna. 1999. *Through the eyes of a child*. Upper Saddle River, NJ: Merrill.

Numeroff, Laura Joffe. 1985. *If you give a mouse a cookie*. Illustrated by Felicia Bond. New York: Harper & Row.

O'Malley, Kevin. 1999. *My lucky hat*. Greenvale, NY: Mondo.

Parish, Peggy. 1963. *Amelia Bedelia*. Illustrated by Fritz Siebel. New York: Harper & Row.

———. 1993. *Thank you, Amelia Bedelia*. Illustrated by Fritz Siebel. New York: Harper Trophy.

Prelutsky, Jack. 1984. *The new kid on the block*. Illustrated by James Stevenson. New York: Greenwillow.

Reading Online. 1997. Newark, DE: International Reading Association.

Sabuda, Robert. 1994. *Tutankhamen's gift*. New York: Atheneum.

School Library Journal. 1961. New York: Cahners.

Schwartz, Alvin. 1982. *There is a carrot in my ear and other noodle tales*. Illustrated by Karen Ann Weinhaus. New York: Harper & Row.

Scieszka, Jon. 1995. *Math curse*. Illustrated by Lane Smith. New York: Viking.

Seuss, Dr. 1957. *The cat in the hat*. New York: Random House.

Something about the author. 1971. Detroit: Gale Research.

Trelease, Jim. 1995. *The read-aloud handbook*. New York: Penguin.

Trivizas, Eugene. 1993. *Three little wolves and the big bad pig*. Illustrated by Helen Oxenbury. New York: Margaret K. McElderry.

Van Allsburg, Chris. 1985. *Polar express*. Boston: Houghton Mifflin.

Zagwyn, Deborah Turney. 1999. *Apple batter*. Berkeley, CA: Tricycle Press.

Zelinsky, Paul O. 1996. *Rumpelstiltskin*. New York: Puffin Books.

Index